Books by Alastair Reid

PASSWORDS

ALASTAIR REID

PASSWORDS

Places, Poems, Preoccupations

An Atlantic Monthly Press Book

LITTLE, BROWN AND COMPANY · BOSTON · TORONTO

LIBRARY OF CONGRESS CATALOG CARD NO. 63-13981

FIRST EDITION

ACKNOWLEDGMENTS

The quotation from Howard Moss is reprinted from "As Sunlight's
Fever" in *A Winter Come, A Summer Gone* (Charles Scribner's Sons,
1960) by permission of Charles Scribner's Sons.

The pieces on Madrid, Gibraltar, Euzkadi, and Barcelona first appeared in *The New Yorker,* and are reprinted here in a slightly modified
form. "Tell Us Where to Go, Guv'nor, and We'll Go" also appeared originally in *The New Yorker,* under the title "The Travellers."

The other prose pieces were published variously in the *Atlantic
Monthly, The Sunday Times, The Queen,* and in *Harper's Bazaar* and
Encounter.

The following poems first appeared in *The New Yorker:* "Speaking a
Foreign Language"; "The Figures on the Frieze"; "Me to You"; "Curiosity"; "Propinquity"; "Wishes"; "What Bones Say"; "The Spiral."

"To a Child at the Piano" is reprinted from the *Listener,* courtesy of
the B.B.C.

The other poems were printed in the *Atlantic Monthly.*

To all of these, acknowledgment is due.

ATLANTIC-LITTLE, BROWN BOOKS
ARE PUBLISHED BY
LITTLE, BROWN AND COMPANY
IN ASSOCIATION WITH
THE ATLANTIC MONTHLY PRESS

*Published simultaneously in Canada
by Little, Brown & Company (Canada) Limited*

PRINTED IN THE UNITED STATES OF AMERICA

For my father

and my son

Fisherman, though I must remain
Merely a tourist in this town,
Consider me for what I am,
A stranger in a lean time.
Your landscape feeds our loneliness.
The sea belongs to both of us.

— HOWARD MOSS

CONTENTS

[xi]

I

I

Notes on Being a Foreigner

I COME suddenly into a foreign city, just as the lamps take light along the water, with some notes in my head. Arriving — the mood and excitement, at least, are always the same. I try out the language with the taxi driver, to see if it is still there; and later, I walk to a restaurant which is lurking round a corner in my memory. Nothing, of course, has changed; but cities flow on, like water, and, like water, they close behind any departure. We come back to confirm them, even although they do not particularly care. Or perhaps we come back to confirm ourselves?

By the time I have finished dinner, I find I have to make an effort to remember the place I left — how it felt, at least.

Matches and toothpaste are the only continuities; once they are used up, the previous existence from which they came has withered and died. I walk along the snowy *quais* in the lamplit dark, breathing a tangle of strangeness and familiarity. Places are a little like old clothes. Wearing them brings nostalgia snowing down. There is both shock and recognition.

How easy it is to fall at once into the habits of a place, most noticeably the eating habits — to dine very late in Spain, to eat heartily in England, to change the whole conception of breakfast, to order certain kinds of drink instinctively. Another country is a new self, I am tempted to say — until I notice all the signs of the old self showing through.

Later, I telephone two or three friends, and am instantly drawn into a web of appointments, talk, question-and-answer, the nowheres of friendship, which supersede language, time, place. And somewhere, one of my friends is saying to someone I do not know yet: "So-and-so is coming for a drink. He is a foreigner."

Natives (an ugly word, but irreplaceable) feel oddly toward foreigners. They may be hostile, aggressive, overfriendly, distant, or possessive; but at least they have the (to them) advantage of being in possession, so that between foreigners and themselves there is a moat with a drawbridge to which they keep the keys. Typical native gambits: "Why, we almost consider you one of us!" Or "What do you think of *our* (railways, king, public lavatories)?" Or "Are you familiar with our expression . . . ?" So much for their feelings. They have the assurance of Being In Possession.

[4]

And the foreigner? It depends on whether he is a foreigner by Necessity, Accident or Choice. One thing, however, is sure: unless he regards being a foreigner as a positive state, he is doomed to be a loser. If he has already chosen not to belong, then all the native gambits are bound to fail. But if he aspires to being a native, then he is forever at the mercy of the natives, down to the last inflexion of the voice.

An expatriate shifts uncomfortably, because he still retains, at the back of his mind, the awareness that he has a true country, more real to him than any other he happens to have selected. Thus, he is only at ease with other expatriates. They justify one another, as they wait about in the sun for the arrival of mail or money. Eventually, they are driven to talk of plumbing, the ultimate sign of the superiority of their own civilization. Whatever they do or write or say has its ultimate meaning for them Back Home. "Yes, but you have to make it in Boston" I once heard from a fanatical expatriate. What's more, he said it in Spanish.

Exiles, as opposed to expatriates, either wither away, or else flourish from being transplanted, depending on whether they keep alive any hope of returning to what they left, or abandon it completely as forever inaccessible. The hope of returning to the past, even at its faintest, makes for a vague unease, a dissatisfaction with the present. The Spanish exiles I have known have been, for the most part, unhappy; Spain, after all, continues to exist, as they are always wistfully aware. The emigrés who left Russia after the Revolution took up, from necessity, another, healthier life, without thinking, and assumed new languages. America has been the most fruitful soil for exiles of all nationalities. America has no time for foreigners as such,

[5]

being too preoccupied with its own tumultuous present, and being aggressively monoglot. If you are there, you are expected to contribute; you cannot just hang about, as you can in the more wistful cities of Europe. In America, you can join, or leave.

Tourists are to foreigners as occasional tipplers are to alcoholics — they take strangeness and alienation in small, exciting doses, and besides, they are well-fortified against loneliness. Moreover, the places they visit expect and welcome them, put themselves out for their diversion. Boredom is the only hazard — it takes a healthy curiosity to keep tourists from rushing home in tears, from sighing with relief at the reappearance of familiarity. The principal difference between tourists and foreigners is that tourists have a home to go to, and a date of departure. I wonder how many of them would confess to have found the pinnacle of pleasure from a trip in the moment of returning home?

How appropriate tourists are, in certain places, at certain seasons! They set off spas, harbours and watering places as pigeons set off cathedrals; they exude an appetite for pleasure and diversion. And often, they bring the best out of the places they visit; women who know they are going to be seen take more trouble with their appearance. The only thing that besets them is that they have to invent reasons for visiting the places they visit, or else suffer from their own pointlessness. And the sun, they discover, is not quite sufficient reason for being anywhere.

A foreigner has a curious perspective on the country he alights in. His foreignness more or less absolves him from being attached to any particular class — his accent puts the natives at rest. It is easier for him to avoid local attitudes and prejudices. He looks at the whole, first, as a game, and then, should he be serious, as an entire human situation. If he cares about it, he develops a calm and attentive eye, a taste for local food, and a passionate dispassion.

"Ah, but, being a foreigner, you cannot possibly know what it is like for us. You cannot suffer." But unless one wants to submerge, to become more English than the English, more German than the Germans, one does know what it is like; and one does suffer. The expatriate settles in a country for peripheral reasons; his involvement is with back home. The foreigner's involvement is with where he is. He has no other home. There is no secret landscape claiming him, no roots tugging at him. He is, if you like, properly lost, and so in a position to rediscover the world, from the outside in.

To be lost, it is not necessary to inhabit a wilderness, nor even to cry.

Belonging. I am not sure what it means, for I think I always resisted it (I still have a crawling terror of being caught in a community sing-song). As for families, they are serviceable social units for a certain time only. With luck, the relationships within them will turn into quite ordinary human ones; otherwise they will wither away. If I belonged to anything, it was to the small, but then enormous, landscapes of my childhood, to houses, trees, gardens, walks — only then was my absorption so utter that I felt no separation between myself and an outside world. Childhood landscapes are an entire containment of mystery — we spend a good part of our lives trying to find

[7]

them again, trying to lose ourselves in the sense in which children are lost. We come away with no more than occasional glimpses, whiffs, suggestions, and yet these are enough, often, to transform suddenly the whole current of our lives. A smell recalls a whole vanished state of being; the sound of a word reaches far back, beyond memory. The beginning of poetry for me was the dazzling realization of all that seemed to be magically compressed into the word "weather."

The sense of oddness, of surprise, of amazement. Occupying places, contexts, languages, we grow used to them. Habit sets in, and they cease to astonish us. In a foreign country, this does not happen, for nothing is exactly recognizable; it has not been with us from our beginnings. The architecture is odd, the shops unexpected; the faces provoke curiosity rather than recognition. And the money — the only real money is the money one knows as a child, for one feels strongly about what it should be worth. Other currencies are play money, coupons; as such, one uses them in a more human, less excruciating way. In a foreign country, the pattern of days is less predictable — each one has its character, and is easier to remember. So, too, the weather; and so, too, the shape and feel of newspapers, the sound of bells, the taste of beer and bread. It is all rather like waking up and not knowing who or where one is. If, instead of simple recognition, one can go through a proper *realization*, then quite ordinary things take on an edge; one keeps discovering oneself miraculously alive. So, the strangeness of a place propels one into life. The foreigner cannot afford to take anything for granted.

In a time like this, it becomes more and more difficult to be lost. It is astonishing into what stark, deserted crevices of the world Coca-Cola signs have found their way. But because we have all begun to look, dress and smell alike, it is still too easy to assume that we are.

Language. To alight in a country without knowing a word of the language is a worthwhile lesson. One is reduced, whatever identity or distinction one has achieved elsewhere, to the level of a near-idiot, trying to conjure up a bed in sign-language. Instead of eavesdropping drowsily, one is forced to look at the eyes, the gestures, the intent behind the words. One is forced back to a watchful silence.

Learning a foreign language is a process of slowly divesting oneself of scaffolding. In the end, something stands up by itself and, if it is lucky, walks away. We lean out desperately to hear how we sound but, alas, we will never know. Not to be able to put oneself into words is the most searing of frustrations; behind the pittering phrases, a huge figure is gesticulating violently. We are suddenly reduced to what we are able to say. And even when we have mastered a language sufficiently well, it keeps trapping us, refusing to allow us to finish a train of thought by deserting us suddenly, making fun of us by coming out wrong. The language we grow up with is our servant; we are always a step ahead of it. A new language, however, already exists; we have to grasp hold of it by the tail, and are never wholly sure where it will take us.

To speak two or three languages is to have two or three totally different selves, like odd suits of clothing. Some fit more easily than others — it is rare to find an American or an Englishman who will speak three languages equally well. As W. H.

Auden remarks, "Like all lovers, we are prejudiced; one may love French, or Italian, or Spanish, but one cannot love all three equally." Even so, I am still aware of having, in Spanish (the language I happen to love), an entirely different personality from my English-speaking one — nor is it simply me-in-translation. I realize this most acutely when I listen to a Spanish friend speaking English. He changes before my ears, and I think, How can I possibly sound to him? "If you knew me in English," I say — but of course, it is impossible. Language, if we care about using it well, rather than efficiently, forever separates us. I have often listened to simultaneous translation between two languages I know well. The meaning? Oh yes, the meaning is there; but it is just *not the same experience.*

Moving between several languages, however, only dramatizes what happens all the time within our own language: whatever our accent, we do not speak in the same voice to a baby, to a clergyman, to an old friend, to a foreigner. The feeling, the wavelengths, act on our voices, and change them. Joyce once remarked, in passing: "Isn't it contradictory to make two men speak Chinese and Japanese respectively in a pub in Phoenix Park, Dublin? Nevertheless, that is a logical and objective method of expressing a deep conflict, an irreducible antagonism." If voices are anything to go by, then the idea of having a fixed, firm self is wildly illusory. We expect those with whom we are in sympathy to listen to what is behind our voice; it is horrifying to have someone listen to nothing more than what we say.

What, really, does it mean to speak in one's own voice? Is there such a voice? Possibly, but I doubt whether it would ever coincide with any of the voices or accents we use, either in public or in private. Nor is it the odd, anonymous voice we hear reading poems to us as we sit silently and attentively in front of them. It is something between a movement of the mind and a way with words, a current, an undertow, slightly beneath the surface of our saying. Nobody's voice, but one's own.

For a writer, it is an invaluable holiday for him to speak, in the course of the day, a language other than the one he writes in. When he comes to use his own language, it seems washed and clean. Kraus remarks: "My language is the universal whore whom I have to make into a virgin." For the foreigner, however, his own language remains steadily virginal.

Children who are bilingual have no difficulty distinguishing between their languages — they associate them with people, and switch quite simply, according to who speaks what. The main problem for people who are genuinely bi- or tri-lingual occurs when they come to write in any one of their languages; they are too used to language as a mechanism by then. Unless they have felt language as mystery (as children do when they repeat a word like "boomerang" endlessly, out of delight), they will never be able to convey a like mystery, and stay stranded in silence.

Ideally, we may arrive at a point of civilization where everybody speaks his own language, and understands everybody else's. Unfortunately, although this can occasionally happen, it feels unnatural. A nuance, a figure of speech, can only provoke another in the same language. The most untidy conversations are those in which too many people know too many languages; they inevitably get out of control. The English are rigorously unsympathetic to foreigners, being excessively proud of their own language. I will never forget a small, lavender-clad Englishwoman standing over her frail collection of luggage at Barcelona airport, waving her scrawny umbrella in the faces of a voluble host of Spanish officials, and snorting, "I don't speak your beastly language!"

Why should we take such an odd pride in being taken for a different nationality from our own? Perhaps because we have succeeded in getting away with an impersonation, in shedding our distinguishing marks. Why should that matter? Anonymity is peculiarly appealing to a foreigner; he is always trying to live in a nowhere, in the complex of his present. To be fastened suddenly to his past may discommode him. Languages are defiant connections to different worlds; as such, they become pressingly important. Still, there is an age after which one can no longer learn new languages, after which the self cannot be extended without danger. New languages can be disappearances, rather than appearances.

"Who are you?" strangers ask, in all innocence, unaware of the enormity of the question. What they are really saying is "Give us a sign." In America, one defines oneself by occupation — "I work for X." In England, one invokes a family. The answers are, however, all deceptions. Nothing would discomfit the questioner more than to have his question taken seriously. Besides, the question really counts only when we ask it of ourselves. Here, to answer "I am a foreigner" in three languages is quite sufficient.

To marry across a difference of language is no more dire than to marry across a difference of temperament; but it can certainly add to the complexities. Explanations are rendered impossible. "Ah, but you don't understand" can become very literal.

The lineaments of travel. To travel far and often tends to make us experts in anonymity — but never quite, for we always carry too much, prepare for too many eventualities. One bag could have been left behind. We are too afraid of unknowns to ignore them.

Airports are the great nowheres of this world; we have made them so. Just as plane trips, be they across oceans or countries, leave nothing to remember but a drone of passing time, so the points of arrival and departure are made to look as alike, as indistinct as possible. Airport restaurants should serve nothing but manna, not tasty but sustaining. The only thing plane trips do for the soul is make it think twice about what it can take with it. Fundamentally, they deceive us by allowing us to travel without a sense of movement.

Sea voyages are meat and drink to foreigners, a mixture of delight and despair, a kind of prelude to dying. The prevailing atmosphere is not exactly one of boredom, but of a limbo almost indistinguishable from it. Every ship has its ministering angels, its characters, its messengers of doom — a row of nuns painted to a bench, a woman with performing dogs, a man who can do tricks with toothpicks. Aboard ship, people are removed from either the contexts they have left or the ones they are going to assume; and this affects them in various ways. For some, it is a relief; for others, a deprivation. Some are impelled to tell the story of their lives, because all at once they have no life, and must create the illusion of what they have left and what is to come. Others wander endlessly along the polished corridors, through the Bamboo Room, the Aquarium Room, listening to the tock of ping-pong, lost. During a sea voyage, a small, artificial community is created, with the intimacy of desperation. One leaves a ship with a flurry of burning addresses which, five minutes after landing, have already turned to ashes. I once heard of a man who spent an entire Atlantic crossing in the bar, playing chess with himself. It made me unaccountably sad.

Trains are for meditation, for playing out long thought-processes, over and over; we trust them, perhaps because they have no choice but to go where they are going. Nowadays, however, they smack of a dying gentility. To travel by car makes journeys less mysterious, too much a matter of the will. One might as easily sit on a sofa and imagine a passing landscape. I doubt whether any truly absorbing conversation ever took place in a car; they are good only for word games and long, tedious narratives. We have come to regard cars too much as appendages of our bodies, and will probably pay for it in the end by losing the use of our legs. We owe to them the cluttering of the landscape, the break-up of villages and towns.

Frontiers fascinate us, for, crossing them, we expect to be metamorphosed — and no longer are. Even although the language changes, the landscape does not.

Nostalgia: leafing through an old passport on a winter evening, trying to remember what we did from stamp to stamp. M. can remember vividly meals we ate in odd places years ago, beds we slept in, conversations we had. I cannot — my memory is sharper for states of mind, atmospheres, weather. It is sad to part with a passport — one has been through so much in its company.

It is not exactly loneliness that afflicts the foreigner, but more that his oddness and experience keep part of him forever separate from every encounter, every gathering, every conversation. Unless he can bear this and see it as something fruitful, however, then he becomes simply lost, an exile without even a country of origin.

Que signifie ce réveil soudain — dans cette chambre obscure — avec les bruits d'une ville tout d'un coup étrangère? Et tout m'est étranger, tout, sans un être à moi, sans un lieu où refermer cette plaie. Que fais-je, à quoi riment ces gestes, ces sourires? Je ne suis pas d'ici — pas d'ailleurs non plus. Et le monde n'est plus qu'un paysage inconnu où mon coeur ne trouve plus d'appuis. Etranger, qui peut savoir ce que ce mot veut dire.

[CAMUS, in his Notebooks.]

Cafés in Europe. The no-man's-lands where people come to take refuge from time and from their outside selves, where waiters blink at anything and understand everything, where people watch one another silently, across all boundaries and frontiers, from behind newspapers with indecipherable headlines. A café is a stage set for an Absolute Nowhere, a pure parenthesis in the swim of time. It provides somewhere for the body to be while the mind wanders; and it also provides an infinity of small dramas, a strange polyglot intermingling of wishes and wavelengths. There, everybody is, by temperament, a foreigner. And to be a foreigner is not, after all, a question of domicile, but of temperament.

[15]

We have weathered so many journeys, and so many forms of love. Would it have been the same, we ask one another, had we stayed still, in the mill with the water running under us? There is no way of knowing.

What haunts a foreigner is the thought of always having to move on, of finding, in the places where he comes to rest, the ghosts he thought were left behind; or else of losing the sharp edge, the wry, surprised eye that keeps him extra-conscious of things. Even at his most assured, he tends to keep a bag packed, in case. The feeling of being lost, however, is never so terrifying when it is compared with the feeling of being found and dried. It is the state of falling in love with a woman one does not quite know yet; and will never quite know.

Foreigners are, if you like, curable romantics. The illusion they retain, perhaps left over from their mysterious childhood epiphanies, is that there might somewhere be a place — and a self — instantly recognizable, into which they will be able to sink with a single, timeless, contented sigh. In the curious region *between* that illusion and the faint terror of being utterly nowhere and anonymous, foreigners live. From there, if they are lucky, they smuggle back occasional undaunted notes, like messages in a bottle, or glimmers from the other side of the mirror.

II

II

Madrid — 1960

THIS morning, under the window, the three everlasting boys have begun their day-long game of soccer; the ball thuds occasionally into one or another of the small gardens, the gates squeak, somebody protests from an upper window, but the game goes on. Soccer, here called *fútbol*, has Madrid in a trance; the local club, Real Madrid, is champion of Europe for the fifth successive year, and the three boys break off their game only to go down to the stadium to catch sight of the players after practice, as they drive away in their Mercedes' and M.G.'s. Maids are calling across from garden to garden, or singing raucously in the washhouses. (In Madrid, either you have a maid or you *are* a maid.) They form a small, separate, gossipy race, like the watchmen, or *serenos*, who clump about at night with sticks and bunches of keys, opening doors for latecomers.

Occasionally the boys call for water, and a maid carries it out to them. Madrid water is supposed to be the best water in the world. Thanks to the rocky soil and the altitude, it has a tangy mineral taste; foreigners are supposed to get drunk on it. Suddenly, a barrel organ appears, mounted on a neat fringed car tugged by a donkey. The organ crashes into a *pasodoble,* and the boys run over to listen. People come out of the houses, carrying children, and coins clink into the pouch on the donkey's harness. Two small girls from next door go off to see if they can borrow a baby. The city is child-mad. "Just put your baby down anywhere," say Madrileños. "Somebody will bring it up." The organ-grinder leaves, and is replaced by a man selling balloons. The maids are now singing the *pasodoble,* all independent of one another. *Plunk!* goes the football. As I leave, I bump into the knife-grinder, who calls every day, even though, on the average, he gets no more to sharpen than a pair of scissors a week.

Out on the street, like a small allegory of Spain, a priest and an Army officer are waiting for the bus; eventually it lumbers up, and the three of us nudge our way on and pay our one peseta eighty céntimos. Two women coming from the market are carrying on a shouted conversation across the bus, through the standing men. Farther down the aisle, a Guardia Civil sways with the rest of us, in his mold-green uniform and flattened tricorne hat, which still has the power to make Spaniards shiver with the memory of the Civil War. Uniform hats have a sinister effect on the faces under them, and this tricorne seems to underline the coldness and cruelty in the long, thin Spanish face. Probably the man hangs up his hat when he is off duty and goes to work as a mason or a carpenter, since most working Spaniards nowadays need two or three jobs to keep going. A man standing beside me is reading *Arriba,* the Falangist newspaper — dull, gray, doggedly faithful to the regime of General Franco, and unwaveringly bland about the state of the world, a great deal of the news of which it neglects to print. Even its football reports are without passion. We blunder past the American Embassy, a neat white locker of a building that Madrileños call *el palomar* (the dovecote), and reach the cafés and shops of the Calle Serrano, where the younger and smarter people go to be seen. Although it is not yet noon, and lunch is at least three hours away, the cafés are half full. The Calle Serrano has a conspicuously well-groomed look — the women are cast in a cool, immaculate mold, and the men are sleek, shaved to the bone, and oddly anonymous behind their sunglasses, which they wear even at night — but the chic of the extravagant leather-and-linen stores has not yet quite eliminated a cubicle-size egg store or a dingy, windowless *marmolería,* where marble is cut and shaped. (Madrid abounds in small, single-minded enterprises. A *candelabrería* makes and repairs cut-glass chandeliers, a *guitarería* does the same for guitars; a *chamarilería* deals in nothing but rags.) A small woman in black is arguing with the bus conductor over her change with such graphic vehemence of expression that the whole bus smiles to itself; anger electrifies the Spanish language. We turn around a great monument, the Puerta de Alcalá, left there by Charles III toward the end of the eighteenth century; it is so vast in its setting that there seems hardly room to pass. Heavily monumented as Madrid is, the scale of its statues is never quite right. Small squares bulge with giants on horseback; the broad Plaza de Colón reduces the figure of Columbus in its center to the proportions of Tom Thumb. A judicious shifting would improve the city no end, but, as Spaniards say at least sixty times a day, "*No hay remedio*" ("What can you do?"). By now, we are in the center of the city, and the traffic has thickened; in Madrid, however, traffic still does not have the terrifying violence of traffic in most large cities but remains good-humored and accommodating. Parking is not yet a problem. Since there are no suburbs, cars go round and round, rather than in and out. I shoulder my way off the bus and start to walk up the broad Paseo de la Castellana, the spine of the city, under the trees. The post-office clock begins its long, chiming preamble to striking noon.

In the shade, people are dawdling and drifting — maids, old men, and occasional soldiers in oversize mud-colored uniforms and huge boots, looking as if they should be anything but soldiers, which is natural enough, since military service is compulsory. An old man in a black beret sleeps deeply on a stone bench. Pigeons are on the scrounge. I stop to buy the newspaper *ABC* at a kiosk well draped with Spanish comic books, French and German papers, and copies of *Life* and *Time* (Spaniards refer to them as *Leafy* and *Teemy*), and then make my way to the café where I am to meet a friend — a painter named Verdejo — at noon; but I do not hurry, since it is unlikely that he will be less than half an hour late. Madrid runs on human time.

The café is cool and gloomy; after the sun, it is difficult to see. Two old men are playing chess by a window. Others are reading newspapers or writing. The place has a quiet, panelled dignity; once the haunt of intellectuals and bullfighters, it is now used mainly by old men, who talk interminably about its past; by young people, who are curious about its reputation; and by painters, who generally remain loyal to their bars. Drinks in Madrid cost more than they did, but the Spanish painters of the moment have become successful, and are richer than they were. I catch hold of the headwaiter, who is so old that he confuses the dead and the living in his mind. He scratches his nose and greets me with the uncertainty of those who know too many people. Has the painter Verdejo been in or left a message? The words and the name take some time to dawn, but, yes, he remembers painfully, Verdejo was here a short while ago, and I must be the gentleman he was to meet, and, yes, he said that he would be about half an hour late. I tell the headwaiter I will have a glass of beer outside, and prepare to wait for Verdejo at least an hour.

The café is more or less in the center of Madrid, and yet the air is quiet enough to allow insects to be heard; the cars whiz rather than roar. The buildings roundabout are gracious, courtly, and bosomy, with large wrought-iron gates and a wealth of trees; the middle part of the city looks like a fat Spanish provincial town, and one can easily imagine horses clattering into the courtyards. In the past twenty years, the city has been spreading to the north, leaving its old selves behind like worm casts. The new part looks more South American than anything else; it is spacious, broad-avenued, and slightly inhuman, with huge, card-house apartment buildings set in dusty, unfinished lots, and new glass-fronted stores and cafeterias. Off to the south and west the old town, with its narrow, crooked, cramped streets, gaslit at night, and its peasant joviality, straggles unevenly around the grubby, graceful Plaza Mayor. The three sections do nothing more than coexist; their architectural attitudes seem forever irreconcilable. Only the vast blue sky of Castile holds them together. One is always aware of the sky — brilliant, intense, wider than any other sky in the world. Under it, the buildings seem to be adrift, the squares and monuments gently afloat.

I take a table near the walk, to watch the people pass. The flow is punctuated regularly by meetings, handshakings, and embraces; all Madrileños appear to be related. The faces suddenly change from graven passivity into flashing lighthouses of zest, and just as suddenly subside. An old woman goes from table to table selling lottery tickets. *"Ultima hora, ultima hora!"* she calls, but the injunction moves nobody. The walkers gawk at me; I gawk back. In Madrid, walking and lounging are the two great estates of being. Those who walk look at the loungers, and those who lounge look at the walkers. Every now and again, a walker will stop and become a lounger, or a lounger get up and walk; the loungers are the fixed points, the walkers the moving context.

All this probably emanates from the fundamental pointlessness of Madrid, which is really a kind of Brasília of yesteryear. In 1561, Philip II decided to make Madrid the capital of Spain, because of its defensibility; it is set in the middle of the arid plateau of Castile, 2372 feet above sea level, two hundred and twenty miles from the nearest sea, and very close to the geographical center of the peninsula. From the air, it looks like a vast overnight camp that has sprawled and stayed; it has no large river to give it a necessary shape, no essential activity to give it a character. Even so, it has been growing tremendously. When the Civil War ended, in 1939, and Madrid set out to rebuild itself, it had a little over a million people; twenty years later, in July, 1959, its two-millionth inhabitant was, as Spanish has it, "given the light." Agricultural workers seep in from the provinces to find jobs in the building trade, which sporadically has been hard at it putting up large developments to house the workers who keep coming in from the provinces to find jobs in the building trade, and so on. The people in the rest of Spain bitterly resent this costly, floating city, set down where no city should sensibly be — there is no doubt that Barcelona would make a much better capital, or even Valencia or Seville — and they resent it not only because they have to feed it and supply it (practically everything eatable comes in from the provinces by truck, through the night, and the fish drivers compete in a continuous mercantile Grand Prix for performance bonuses) but also because they have to wait unendurably long for every kind of official permission to come from the capital, which houses all the government Ministries and the head offices of the banks and industries. The old people in the provinces reputedly shake their fists in the direction of Madrid, their Mecca of frustration, before going to bed. Nevertheless, what Madrid says goes.

A young waiter rushes across with my beer, fifteen minutes after I asked for it, and I turn to the newspaper. *ABC* has the largest circulation (about eighty thousand) of Madrid's three morning papers, and is monarchist in outlook. It attends to present events with the air of a faithful butler who hopes someday to come into a legacy, yet, like practically all Spanish papers, it lacks any crisp sense of immediacy; it has a limp, month-old air. Free, independent reporting is unknown in Spain; the news is heavily censored, and events that might in any way reflect on the stability of the regime are simply not mentioned. *ABC's* life lies in its stylistic extravagance; it quivers with rhetorical flourishes and metaphorical flights, especially on the sports and obituary pages. Today's front page singles out some recent remarks by the British Foreign Minister: "England and Spain have many common interests. For example, last year, three hundred and fifty thousand English holidayed in Spain, and it seems reasonable to try to better relations between the two countries." The newspaper adds a shy, pleased comment.

In 1945, as the Second World War ended, the British gesticulated angrily in Franco's direction before they hung up their rifles, and on March 4, 1946, Britain, France, and the United

States issued a joint declaration based on the hope that "leading patriotic and liberal-minded Spaniards may soon find means to bring about a peaceful withdrawal of Franco, the abolition of the Falange, and the establishment of an interim or caretaker government under which the Spanish people may have an opportunity freely to determine the type of government they wish to have, and to choose their leaders." Now, however, the weather in the outside world has changed considerably, and General Franco receives a lot of cordial visitors. The United States maintains a handful of important military bases in Spain, and in December, 1959, President Eisenhower drove amicably through Madrid with General Franco and was goggled at admiringly by thousands of Spaniards, who had not seen so substantial a foreign personage in ages. (Absolute moral values scarcely belong in international politics and economics. For every tourist who feels queasy about setting foot in Spain there are hundreds who rush in with gusto. So do we grow used to the relative nature of things.) General Franco patiently waited out the years of his disfavor abroad, and now he can lay claim to having been the original anti-Communist. He has hated the Communists ever since they fought against him in the Civil War, and in his eyes the Western powers have come around to his point of view, waking up a few years ago to find him their staunch ideological ally, if a strange bedfellow.

In Spain itself, not much has changed; since 1939 the country has been a dictatorship under the direct rule of General Franco — a police state, with no civil rights and no legal political opposition. Its economy lags drastically behind that of the rest of Europe, and even though Spaniards are capable of absorbing poverty more cheerfully than any other people, the fact remains that the vast majority of the population of thirty million are miserably poor. Political imprisonment continues in waves, and there is active censorship of books, films, and newspapers. The summing-up of Spain grows sorrier as it grows longer, and yet, given all these disagreeable political realities, Spain has a vivacious, warm, and thriving personal life to it, a gaiety, a spontaneous joy; it is far from cowed. Spaniards regard themselves as conspirators happily brought together by a common enemy; no attack on the regime from outside ever approaches in virulence the denunciations they make in private. "What do you think of Franco?" asks a foreign correspondent of a Madrid reporter. "Sh-h-h, we can't talk here," the reporter replies, looking nervously around the bar. "Let's go somewhere else." After skulking across Madrid, they reach a deserted garden in the Retiro Park. "Well?" says the correspondent. "Sh-h-h!" whispers the reporter. "You see — *I like him!*" The most puzzling fact of all is that Spaniards have endured General Franco for so long and have been able, for all their passionate intensity, to shrug him off.

A week ago, I sat in the same café talking with a middle-aged surgeon, a shrewd, spry man with whom I occasionally play tennis, and I asked him to tell me why Spain still sat obediently under General Franco's thumb.

"You got me on a good day," he said. "Yesterday I was very sad. Tomorrow is a holiday, and so I would be flippant and cynical. Today you let me win at tennis, so I will tell you the truth."

This I doubted. The truths and pronouncements of Spaniards form a great morass of contradiction; like the battery of Spanish proverbs, they pin down in a stray moment a whole that, in its shifting turbulence, can never be pinned down. Anyway, heartened by the tennis, my friend proceeded to answer my question seriously, and at length.

"I am glad you are not an economist or a sociologist," he said.

[27]

"Otherwise, you would collect endless statistics on Spain, which would all lead to disastrous conclusions, and then you would begin saying, 'What Spain needs is this' and 'What Spain must do is that,' and you would be lost, because we would not do it. You cannot get anywhere without understanding our character, the way we are. You must have noticed how much we talk — we stay up till three every morning talking. We have *sobremesas* [an odd Spanish word that means just sitting around talking after meals] twice a day. Besides, we meet friends in cafés before lunch and before dinner, and we talk until our faces hurt. You see, for us talking is a kind of illusory action. We have no freedom of speech in a constitutional sense, so we indulge ourselves in speaking freely past the danger point, and now talk is our substitute for doing *anything*. We talk away our love affairs, the books we could have written, the revolutions we should have organized. You see, we are all paralyzed. Our Civil War shocked us to a point where we *dread* action. It was so fratricidal — no, suicidal — that after it we were unable to feel anything. You saw it as a war of ideologies; for us it was a war of allegiances. We all fought it in our own heads, and we all lost, with the exception of Franco. And everything that has happened since is *our* responsibility, because we have let it happen.

"In Spain, we could never be democratic, as the United States is. No two of us can ever agree. Look at our history, particularly the history of the Republic, and you will see that we have never been capable of collective action; we have only moved through the influence of persuasive individuals, who have always generated even more persuasive opponents. We grow up with polarities. We are Catholics at the beginning, and then we turn on the Church and become savagely anti-clerical, although our good friends — our brothers, even — are priests. Then we become atheists (you know that old Spanish joke, 'I'm an atheist, thank God'), but our whole manner of looking at things remains Catholic — our sense of sin, our feeling of doom, our moral rigidity. The enormous weight of the past of Spain hangs over us, and we ridicule it and try to live extravagantly in the present, but we never get rid of our cumbersome destiny. We laugh at everything and find everything laughable, and are sentimental about our families and our dogs, and yet at the same time we are proud and violent and cold and cruel. Often, when nobody is looking and when I am upset, I kick my dog, and the next minute I comfort him. You know, too, how authoritarian we are, and yet we hate authority. We are Don Quixote and Sancho Panza at once. We take everything seriously and can no longer be serious about anything. We are all these things and yet no one of them, except at odd moments. To the inside of our backbones we are anarchists. In Spain, you cannot speak of masses — we are thirty million separate people. You see how impossible it is for us to want anything? Whatever happens is quite enough for us! You think that Franco has done enough to unite us against him? You forget that Franco, too, is a Spaniard. He does not have intelligence; he has more — he has a peasant's intuition, which never fails him, and he has been trained as a soldier. He does not act; he reacts. When something goes dangerously wrong, he puts his finger in the wall. Another hole — another finger! He has never had any policy, and so we have had nothing to oppose; since he has given us no future, we have nothing tangible enough to alter. We just go on. You see, he is our doom, and against him we discover ourselves, but only personally. And he does hold us together; without him we would have to decide *ourselves* what we want, and that we are incapable of doing."

"But now a whole generation has grown up in Spain without the memory of the Civil War," I said.

"True enough," the surgeon replied, "but the Spain they have grown up in has been so dingy, so cramped, so confused that all they want to do is to leave it. Or, if they stay, they want only more money, more pleasure, more cars, more movies. They don't know how to think, and we have neither encouraged nor inspired them. We no longer have any heart for a struggle. We have only our families, our friends, and our work. I know that we sound ludicrous, but, my dear fellow, we are tragic."

Political speculation in Spain is a kind of game that the gentlemen are supposed to play after dinner. The talkers remain as distinct from their convictions as chessplayers from their chessmen; they have played together for a long time, and know one another's game. The political opposition to Franco is intelligent, but it has splintered into many factions. The Communists make much capital out of Franco's hatred of them, but they prefer to wait until things get worse. The Socialists have been the most active party and, of late, the most frequently imprisoned. The six or seven small democratic parties keep looking for a common platform, but they are bound together mostly by despair. The Catholic Action group has been outspoken, but it gets little support from the workers, to whom it addresses itself; they feel they have nothing to gain from joining anything, and a great deal to lose. The monarchist parties have turned into bands of steady hopers. Odd groups left over from the Republic flicker away. But since none of these parties exist legally, and since arrests quickly follow any signs of overenthusiasm, the stand taken by any of them is doomed to be largely theoretical. The Falange, or Fascist party, though it still stands solidly behind the regime, and in a sense *is* the regime, is no longer as personally favored by Franco as it once was. It is not just that the Falangists are clumsy and heavy-handed; for Franco to be identified now as head of the Falange is what we would call bad public relations, something to which the General has grown surprisingly sensitive.

Actually, one of the most influential groups in Spain is not a political party but an organization called Opus Dei, which was founded in 1928 by a rich Spanish priest, José María Escrivá de Balaguer, and has since mushroomed all over the world. Its aim is to exercise a pervasive influence for good, and it has had tremendous success in Spain because its manner of action is much more intelligently fitted to the Spanish situation than that of the political parties. The workings of Opus Dei are shrouded in Masonic secrecy, but it is thought to have about ten thousand members, most of them intellectuals — professors, editors, publishers, priests, economists, professional men, Cabinet Ministers, students. Full-fledged members, or *numerarios*, take vows of poverty, chastity, and obedience, and most of them turn their earnings over to Opus Dei. In theory, it aims at a blend of spiritual and professional perfection; members are expected to remain in the world, devoting their professional energies to a religious end. ("Never go into details of your apostolate unless it be for someone else's benefit," cautions its handbook, *Camino*, which was written by its founder, and reads like an odd blend of Lord Baden-Powell and Nietzsche.) Priests are not at all predominant in Opus Dei; infiltration into, not withdrawal from, the world is the plan. Recruiting goes on with an evangelical directness reminiscent of the Oxford Group. There is money aplenty and, by now, a substantial amount of power. Opus Dei has control, more or less, of a chain of cinemas, a publishing house, a literary magazine, most of the public information agencies, the evening paper *Madrid,* and the Banco

Popular. Even beyond that, its influence, through certain individuals, is very strong. In Franco's Cabinet, the Minister of Commerce, Alberto Ullastres, is a full member, and three other Cabinet Ministers are sympathizers. It would seem that Opus Dei has the ear of Franco, if only because he can count on the incorruptibility of its adherents. In a Spanish Cabinet Minister, incorruptibility is something.

Madrileños have taken to crediting Opus with control of everything from soccer to the weather. The group professes no political aims — in itself a comment on the impotence of political parties in Spain. Like the Church, it is certainly planning to survive Franco without any difficulty. It is, however, an élite, and both the Church and the Catholic Action group are suspicious and jealous of it. Some of its pronouncements have a familiar superman ring to them, and since its pursuit of power is relentlessly successful and its silence is absolute, it has, as Spaniards say, "to be watched with both eyes." The members of Opus have at least been intelligent enough to see that in Spain a powerful individual in the right place is worth infinitely more than a hundred platforms.

In all this muddle, the least unfeasible prospect is that of restoring the monarchy. Franco has made several feints, over the years, that show he has entertained the possibility of his own mortality and would not be unwilling to step down in favor of a king. Don Juan, the pretender to the Spanish throne, whose father, Alfonso XIII, abdicated in 1931, has had several meetings with Franco. Temperamentally and sentimentally, Spaniards hanker after a king, and they would take to one all the more gladly if it meant the disappearance of Franco. Four years ago, the plan was to groom Don Juan Carlos, the son of Don Juan, for the succession, but since the grooming was to be undertaken by Franco and his advisers, popular enthusiasm was only moderate. More recently, rumor has had it that Don Juan himself would take over quite soon, but rumor seems to have had it wrong. The aristocracy quivers with excitement at the thought of another king. The people will wait and see. The best thing to be said for a constitutional monarchy is that it would settle the problem of Franco's successor without throwing Spaniards back into the chaos of having to organize themselves, and, in the long run, would more easily accomplish the weaning that Spain needs before it can take charge of itself. The people have been saturated for years with the propaganda of the regime, and the country is not now in a condition that would permit free elections to be called overnight. But again, speculation aside, the decision rests on the whim of Franco, and, as Spaniards know well, he has a whim of iron.

The Spanish economy is in such a fix that its improvement must take precedence over everything else, even over things political. By 1958, the economic situation looked desperate; the peseta was slipping, trade payments were seriously unbalanced, prices kept rising, public money was being wasted on fruitless building, agriculture was in the doldrums, and industry was hopelessly encumbered by government controls. Then, quite suddenly, in July, 1959, the Minister of Commerce, Ullastres, announced the beginning of a new stabilization program, to create "hard" money and to restore a favorable trade balance. At the same time, Spain became a member of the European Economic Community and got promises of support from the World Bank, the International Monetary Fund, and various private banks in the United States. Madrileños smiled wryly. Ullastres made enthusiastic speeches about his New Deal; meanwhile, bank credits were cut, small industry took a hard knock, and unemployment rose. Yet, bit by bit, exports began to pick up, the trade and payment balances began to show positive, and the peseta began to stay firm. The government went through the motions of withdrawing some controls from industry, and then actually did remove some of the obstacles to foreign investment. As time passed, the plan fulfilled itself to the letter; in July of 1960 Spain had an almost incredible foreign credit of three hundred and fifty million dollars, and the more economically sophisticated European countries have been loud in their praise.

On paper, everything looks fine, but in order for this stabilization to have any meaning it must be followed by what economists call "reactivation," and for Spain this is another matter. To get close to anything resembling a market economy, where people make things and consume them and the country prospers, Spain must practically begin again. The labor laws need vigorous revision, for clumsy labor syndicates now wield the power that the workers themselves should have, and there is no free employment. Government agencies still bear down heavily on industrial organization. Building has come to a standstill, since, for the sake of creating hard money, government spending had to be controlled. Moreover, many of the more powerful Spanish businessmen are opposed to a competitive economy and to the coming of foreign capital, since it would trim their profits drastically. It is easy enough to see coolly what needs to be done in Spain, and even to insist logically that it must be done, but the moves are so drastic, so full of liberal implications, that Franco is unlikely to let them be made in any earnestness. It suits his book much better to slip gently back into inflation, which is more immediately palliative. A bouncing economy needs a reliable future; because Franco refuses to grant one, nobody else cares to take a chance on it. With the country waiting for a change as a seismographer might wait for an earthquake or a saint for a miracle, no one feels much like investing in anything, even in time. And if the economy falters again, Franco is cheerfully confident that the money will come from somewhere. It always has.

General Franco's method of running Spain has been to give every man his ear but none his voice. He remains bland, owlish, and apparently adaptable; the about-turns in his public pronouncements would shame a candidate for an obscure office. He picks favorites and favorite groups, programs, and policies as it suits him, never allowing himself to become closely identified with any one of them for long, never letting any one of them grow too strong. As Commander-in-Chief of the Army, and in view of his relations with the Church, he needs no party. The Church gives his regime an appearance of respectability and solidity; the regime, in return, gives the Church freedom to pursue its activities. An enlightened Spanish priest, though — and there are many — is in an even more difficult position than an enlightened layman; the weight of authority, temporal and spiritual, is apt to make his enlightenment an insupportable burden. As for the Army, it has long ceased to be an army in a military sense. Along with the police, it forms the symbol and agency of Franco's absolute power, yet its own power is neither succinct nor clear enough to allow it to act for itself, or for interests other than Franco's; it remains anxious and obedient. By judiciously doing and saying practically nothing, Franco has kept the air about him quivering, or at least stirring, with possibility. As long as he may move, he makes it difficult for anyone to be convinced that he never will. "Nobody could *be* like that," Spaniards say, "but Franco is."

Since Franco exists and is accepted as a kind of Fate, Spaniards have diverted their passions into their personal lives, and they have an astonishing appetite for diversion; they are quite prepared to go *en famille* to anything at all — cinemas, football matches, bullfights, cockfights, jai alai, races of all kinds — and they go not as spectators or fans but as critics. If a team plays well, they clap their appreciation; if a bullfighter is lethargic or incompetent, they jeer and whistle. The judgment, they feel, is in their hands. They grumble and applaud in the movies, which most of them attend once a week. (In Spain, there is one cinema seat for every 7.4 people, or more than twice the percentage in the United States; the films are mostly American, censored, and dubbed — apparently by a small group of Spaniards, since Marlon Brando and Fred Astaire turn up with identical voices.) The theatre is moribund; the plays that run are domestic farces, funny enough but endlessly reiterative and full of family jokes. One theatre puts on bowdlerized Tennessee Williams. ("A puzzling man," the critic for *ABC* has remarked.) Civic culture is not Madrid's strong point; it has preferred to stay personal. The hunger of Spaniards for sport and competition can be oddly gruesome; in spring the city staged races in the Retiro Park for wheelchairs, complete with timers, judges, cups, and, of course, invalid drivers.

A while ago, a friend of mine arrived in Madrid eagerly predisposed to see a bullfight after some months in New York of bullfight movies, bullfighters' biographies, and learned articles on bullfights in glossy magazines. We went, on a Sunday afternoon, to Las Ventas, the larger of Madrid's two bull rings. Twelve or thirteen thousand people, mainly German, Scandinavian, and English, filled the ringside seats. The upper terraces were sparsely sprinkled with Spaniards, who quickly moved down when the fight began. The plaza was no more than half full. The *corrida* itself proved not so much mediocre as indifferent; the bulls were substantial and brave enough, but they tired quickly, and the matadors, all of them veterans, mostly stayed aloof, not really trying to dominate or control the bulls. Although enough of the ritual gesture of the art was left to let any visitor say squarely to his diary, "I saw a bullfight," everything — bulls, matadors, spectators, and weather — seemed heavy with ennui, and the afternoon, yawning and dwindling out, scarcely raised a whistle. Bullfights are like melons, an implacable Spanish proverb maintains; you never know what they are going to be like until you get inside. To judge by that *corrida,* melon growers cannot be too enthusiastic over the analogy.

The bullfight, as an institution, is having difficulties. It still hits high points; one afternoon last May, during San Isidro, Madrid's week of fiesta, Antonio Ordoñez, the indubitable No. 1, fought coolly and majestically, in pouring rain, and cut two ears. (Madrid, arrogantly, never awards more for a great performance, while lesser rings in the provinces will give a bullfighter ears, tail, and hoof on good days.) The rest of the week was unrelieved tedium — road-company bullfighting. Nothing is sorrier than a bad or indifferent bullfight; irritation replaces catharsis. A bullfighter, to be good, needs a limited, intense, knowledgeable crowd that understands bulls and is able to encourage a matador beyond himself and keep him true. When Manolete was fatally gored, in 1947, he had, single-handed, set impossibly high standards; he had worked closer to the bull, claimed greater fees, and acquired a more heroic public personality than any bullfighter before him. Unfortunately, succeeding generations of bullfighters — and their managers — have tended to think more of money, publicity, and a prolonged career than of the purity of their art. In so tenuous, finely balanced, and personal an art, love must come before money. Instead, Safety First is now the motto of most bullfighters; they

[37]

live to fight another day. A few, like Ordoñez, are devoted and absorbed enough to take trouble; they are still, from time to time, inspired — the occasions are not predictable — and, from time to time, gored.

Tourists have to share the blame. They were shut out of Spain from 1936 until 1947, and could not travel easily until much later, but they now pour in, hot after the romantic image of Old Spain — bullfights, fiestas, flamenco dancing, wineskins, and windmills. (Actually, Spain goes to less bother for its tourists than any other country I can think of. Old Spain has not been cynically contrived, like Olde England.) The bullfight is high on the list of Spanish Experiences, and the tourists and the international set have, together, kept bullfighting in full swing. It is quite easy for the shrewd matador appearing before several thousand palpitating foreigners to fight with a flourish, to look graceful and brave, without working the bull or running much risk; the foreigners' applause will drown the jeers and whistles of the Spaniards. Without tourists, the onetime national fiesta would continue on a smaller and purer scale; it cannot become a business, or even a regular spectacle, without succumbing to shady practices, which abound, and losing its soul. The best bullfights happen in the provinces, at local fiestas. There, Spaniards attend with passion; in the cities, they go wistfully two or three times a year, when they can afford it, to see if it is *really* as bad as they fear. Many times, in the café, I have listened to indignant, day-long conversations about the decline of the bulls, which are usually led by a little wizened monkey of a man who was once a member of Manolete's *cuadrilla*. "When *el maestro* was alive," he growls, "the ring was a church, not a countinghouse, and we worshipped the bulls and cried as we killed them. Look at these *toreros* nowadays. They're scientists and robbers, and the *público* applauds every time they take off their hats! Far better to have rubber bulls with motors in them. We have disgraced ourselves. Manolete would have wept for shame!"

Some days after I had taken my New York friend to the bullfight, I asked him to come with me to a nighttime soccer match — a European Cup semifinal between Real Madrid and Barcelona, its sharpest Spanish rival. We arrived twenty minutes early — allowing time to rent cushions (the seats are of concrete) and to settle ourselves — but the stadium, which holds upward of a hundred and twenty-nine thousand people with surprising grace and ease, was already overflowing, and it was difficult to speak above the steady, muted screech of the crowd. There was not a German or a Scandinavian in sight. The game was breathtakingly fast, brilliant, clean, and spectacular, and the crowd was hungrily attentive. Madrid won by three goals (scored by an Argentine and a Hungarian) to Barcelona's one (scored by another Hungarian), and the city was in a state of limp joy. Diners and waiters replayed the game over soup; bus drivers discussed it with policemen at red lights. Not long afterward, Real Madrid went on to win the final, in Glasgow, and when the team returned in triumphal procession from the airport, a crowd almost as vast as the one that had turned out to look at President Eisenhower roared its joy. The euphoria in the city quite obliterated any anxiety over U-2 and the failure of the summit. "Yes, yes," people said, "but *we* won the Cup."

At the moment, football rivets the attention of the greater part of the Spanish people — even small provincial towns throb with it — for nothing else allows them to feel so justifiably superior to the rest of Europe. Real Madrid is a valuable property. It plays numerous friendly games all over Europe, for a fee of between thirty and forty thousand dollars a game, and has been able to buy star players from just about everywhere. Its regular team includes Hungarians, Brazilians, Argentines, and Uruguayans, but only one Madrileño. The stadium is soon to be enlarged to hold a hundred and sixty thousand; at the moment, it seldom has a crowd of less than ninety thousand. In Madrid, the players are as newsworthy as the British Royal Family in England; if the wife of one of them has a child, the news gets a headline in the press. Newspaper reports of games are meditative, heroic, poetic; *Marca*, the sports daily, recently noted the weight lost by each player during a game, and added, for its more thorough readers, the total weight loss of the team.

Just after the failure of the May, 1960, summit, General Franco, as a gesture of sympathy to his friend President Eisenhower, cancelled two football matches that Spain was due to play against Russia. He has done many worse things, but nothing recently that has brought him such unpopularity, for he did away with a chance to solidify Spain's prestige in the one area where the country has made a perceptible dent in the outside world. When, as a result of this action, the European Football Federation threatened for a time to ban Spain from international competition, the people howled. It was a grave slip on Franco's part. Football has steadily and successfully diverted the attention of the multitude from political realities, and he should have known better than to mix the two things.

By now, an hour has passed, and the café is full to its edges, but there is still no sign of Verdejo. I decide to give him fifteen minutes more. Two or three friends have passed, and one has given me his card, with a new address. (Spaniards exchange calling cards as readily as they shake hands. After two or three parties, you are left with the makings of a small professional directory.) Although it is easy enough in Madrid to find doctors, plumbers, bullfight tickets, and business connections in the ordinary way, no Madrileño would ever dream of doing so; he consults his cards and his friends for a direct personal connection. "I think my brother-in-law could help you," someone is likely to say. Or "It happens that a cousin of my wife's is in charge of that office." Or "Do mention my name." Everyone in Madrid must mention everyone else at least once a week. Obligations and favors form a kind of currency, like unwritten IOUs, and every Spaniard, since his personal honor is involved, will go to endless trouble to find connections for his friends. To countries with a higher degree of bureaucratic sophistication, Spain seems hopelessly corrupt; Spaniards retort that these countries are inhuman. Loyalty to friends, they argue, is infinitely more valuable than loyalty to a system.

"It must be hard on those people who don't know anybody," I remarked to a lawyer.

He looked at me oddly. "*Everybody* knows *somebody*," he said.

There is, however, another side to the coin — less human, less innocent, less jovial. It would be foolish to imagine that General Franco runs Spain single-handed, especially since Spain prickles with a steady resentment. His personal power is impressively final, but, as it deploys itself downward, it has to be administered by floating legions of police and bureaucrats, and maintained by inspectors, motorcyclists, and streetsweepers. General Franco appears in public in a wide range of uniforms, and, in consequence, each minion on duty wears something of his sinister aura. Since nobody has been able to lick Franco, a great many people have joined him, propelled by either ambition or greed. The payoffs of public position are not to be sneezed at, and the sharpness of moral responsibility has been rubbed away by the passage of time. In government offices, the portrait of the Caudillo looks down benevolently on his servants; even he can hardly be aware of the multiplicity of sins that are committed in his name.

In the swirl of traffic, two boys on bicycles are riding in file, with a chandelier tinkling and swaying on a long pole slung between them. They balance with an airy nonchalance; it looks easy. A German with a briefcase asks if I am using the other chair; I say that I hope to be. Just at that moment, Verdejo arrives, mopping his bald head (Spaniards seem to go emphatically bald at a stroke) and smiling. I remind him that he is late, but he merely spreads his hands, and then sits down and claps for the waiter.

"Bring us a bottle of Valdepeñas and a melon at once," he tells him, and then says to me, "Listen, I have had the most emotional morning. I have been with an American in the Prado, and he has bought a very large painting of mine. This is what I am celebrating."

"But at the moment you have no paintings." I had been in his studio only a few days previously, and I recalled its dramatic bareness.

Verdejo waves his hand. "He is coming to the studio in two days. I have described the painting to him, and I see it myself so clearly. Two nights of work . . . What's more, he is taking me to the bullfight this afternoon — you, too, if you wish — and later to dinner. And I have just given him an hour's lecture on Goya. The Prado should employ me. I can even describe the paintings in the cellars. You know, it is an iceberg, that museum; the bulk of it is in the cellar. So we will all go to the bulls, no?"

"I was thinking of going to the football."

"*Ka*, you have no soul, you insult us. But listen. You must explain to me about Americans. This one is mad. All he does is talk about Spain, how beautiful Spain is, how human Spain is, how he wants to give up everything — his *negocios* — and live in Spain. He must be an *idiota!* Who would *want* to live here, in this terrible city? We have no *mystique,* no meaning, no money, no art, no music. We are all peasants and liars. All we have is long tongues and discontent; thin, frustrated men and fat, placid women. By all means, let us *give* Spain to the Americans."

"Where would *you* go?" I ask him.

"Go? Oh, we wouldn't go. We must stay here and see that nobody changes anything. You worry about Franco? *Pouf,* he is a hangnail, a carbuncle; he will pass. You keep saying we have to change; everybody tells us we're bound to change. Why should we? We are of inestimable value. We know how to live better than anyone, and that's what this American wants from us. Look at us here. We're sitting here in the sun, aren't we? We're going to the bulls, aren't we? I've sold a painting that I haven't painted — is that not brilliant? And here comes the melon and the wine — is that not a miracle? You don't understand that we live by miracles. Am I not always telling you about *el milagro español?* My poor friend, why should you always be wanting us to make sense? Do miracles make sense?"

I spread my hands. We give each other up, as we always do.

Verdejo takes out a small silver pocketknife and begins to slice the melon. "Did I ever tell you?" he says. "In Spain, we have a most amusing saying that has it that melons are like bullfights — you never know what they're going to be like till you get inside. Wine?"

Gibraltar — 1961

G IBRALTAR, as all schoolboys and insurance men know, is
not so much a place as a thing — a positive monument to
durability. Oaths are readily sworn, and vows taken, on the
assumption of its continuing existence. I saw Gibraltar often
enough, during the war and after, without ever paying much
attention to it beyond realizing that if anything would keep, it
would be the Rock, but more recently I began to brood on the
implausible fact of a British Crown Colony's existing on Spanish soil, for if ever two temperaments were unlikely to blend
they are the English and the Spanish. So I decided to fly down
one Sunday from Madrid, along with a smattering of American
tourists who were catching a ship, three rawboned British
businessmen, and a solitary, black-eyed Gibraltarian. At the
Madrid airport, the Spanish police stamped our passports with

a fixed official scowl, which did not surprise me — the resentment felt by Spain over Gibraltar is curiously sharp, considering it has been a British possession for over two hundred and fifty years. I have noticed that while the more sophisticated Spaniards dismiss "the Gibraltar question" airily as one of little importance, they always add, as a rueful afterthought, "Of course, it really *is* ours, you know!"

Gibraltar is whimsically small (it could be set down in Central Park, with some spilling over at the edges), but its situation and its blunt burliness lend it a pugnacious emphasis — it forms a kind of thumb on the eastern tip of the Bay of Algeciras, and misses being an island by dint of a narrow isthmus joining it to Spain. As English schoolboys can tell you, it was one of the Pillars of Hercules, and a gatepost of the entrance to the Mediterranean; from it you can easily see the looming African coast, a mere twenty miles to the south, and the neat white Spanish town of Algeciras, across the bay to the west. Its air of spunky self-confidence comes in part from its being an autonomous British Crown Colony — the smallest one in the Commonwealth — with its own colonial government, its own stamps and police force, its own little frontier. To look at, the Rock is quite monumental, towering sheer up from the flat table of the airport to a height of almost fourteen hundred feet, pitted silver-gray, with occasional green wooded shelves. Its presence imposes a dwarfish proportion on the town of Gibraltar, which sprawls up its western side (the eastern side is only sparsely populated), and one finds oneself regularly glancing up at its brooding, changing bulk. It is so emphatically there, and time has endowed it with a great-grandfatherly aura.

A bus set me down in the middle of the town, and I asked the driver if the hotel was far. "Not at all," he replied. "I'm afraid nothing is far here." He was quite right. One finds oneself walking back and forth along Main Street several times a day, in the hope that it may actually be longer than it is, and I noticed also that after two or three days I began to be conscious of having seen a great many of the people before. With so little flat ground at the foot of the Rock, the town has had to clamber over itself to exist at all; the houses perch on one another's shoulders, and in the steeper streets you look from your basement window into your neighbor's attic. Fundamentally, the town has a Spanish look, with faded pink-and-brown walls, but on top of this has been imposed a brisk, shipshape British tidiness — a thoroughly un-Spanish spickness of fresh paint, lampposts, notices, and polished brass. Also, I had arrived on a Sunday, but it was far from being the lazy, garrulous Spanish Sunday I was used to; instead, the town was shut up in tight disapproval, with not a shop open and the streets haunted by idling sailors gazing aimlessly at windowfuls of silent cameras and watches — British sailors, to be sure, doomed to such shuttered Sundays ashore. As I came down at dusk from a long, climbing walk, a solid English hymn was manfully emanating from the Cathedral, but around another corner or two a cha-cha-cha was having its way in a grubby dance hall. In Gibraltar, you necessarily grow used to juxtapositions of this kind. The place is so many things at once — a fortress, a seaport, an international market, a British colonial capital, a place where people live, a fragment of Spain — and the representatives of these separate functions jostle one another comically and continuously. Stiff-faced service officers, gawking tourists with wallets and cameras cocked, Spanish workmen shuffling in from La Línea de la Concepción — the Spanish town at the top of the isthmus — for day labor, shopkeepers smiling expansively in their doorways, and retired English squires with tweedy dogs all mingle in buzzing coexistence. As far as the town goes, it is first a fortress. The massive gray walls and the names of the streets — Castle Ramp, Engineer Lane, Line Wall Road, Casemates Square, Bomb House Lane, King's Bastion, South Barrack Road — all smack of siege; an occasional sentry with fixed bayonet glares into space, and faraway bugle calls float up from the harbor. One morning, I ran into the changing of the Governor's Guard, a small pomposity in itself, with an apoplectic sergeant major wrenching words of command from his apparently exhausted lungs; simultaneously, a stunted Spaniard, with beret and yellow cigarette end, teetered across the square behind a wheelbarrow of fish, calling *"Pescado!"* in a quavering tenor. I felt I had stumbled into the rehearsal of some strange multilingual musical. If I had waited about long enough, the English-looking policeman on the corner might have burst into flamenco, as he did on other occasions.

Eventually, it dawned on me that this apparent English-Spanish ambiguity was quite normal and that Gibraltarians are not only comfortably bilingual but quite distinct in character from both British and Spaniards. The British, for the most part, are attached either to the garrison or to the administration for a particular tour of duty, and seem to speak little Spanish; Spaniards come across the frontier — eleven thousand of them every day — to work in the dockyard or in hotels and restaurants, returning to Spain each evening. The Gibraltarians are the only ones who truly *live* in Gibraltar, and they form just over two thirds of the population of twenty-six thousand. They are, both technically and passionately, British subjects, but at the same time, as they point out, Gibraltar is not Britain. "We are sometimes referred to as being embarrassingly British," one of them told me over a drink at his house, "but we are so out of respect, and also because it has been entirely in our interest to claim our British nationality — we have absorbed so much, and we have acquired our whole civic organization from the British, even to the extent of imposing income tax on ourselves. But at the same time, as far as our feelings for Britain go, it's like having a foster mother. We are, at bottom, more concerned with our distinctiveness than we are with being British. We tend to make fun of any Gibraltarian who becomes in our eyes too English, but at the same time you will scarcely find one of us who is not thankful for his British passport."

"But do you not feel strong attachments to Spain — temperamentally, I mean?" I asked him.

"Oh, tremendously," he said. "We are very much at home in Spain; in fact, I would say that we count entirely on Spain for our pleasure. Every time I can get away in summer, I drive to the *ferias* — I have a great passion for the bulls, and at the bull-fight I react like a Spaniard. But remember, we Gibraltarians are also realistic. When we take a look at Spain economically and politically, we thank our stars for Gibraltar. We love going to Spain, but when we return, we feel that we are returning to freedom. There is not one of us who would choose to become a Spaniard now — we'd rather be Chinese. We are both British and Spanish, but we are neither. We eat both *potaje* and eggs-and-bacon; we listen to flamenco and to military bands. You notice that we speak both languages equally badly — in fact, we scarcely realize which one we are speaking. My father was a Gibraltarian, but my mother was Spanish, and, as a child, when I wanted to annoy her, I used to speak English."

At that point, the telephone rang and he picked it up. "*Hola, qué tal? . . . Sí, pasa por aquí* about four o'clock," he said into it.

I saw what he meant. In time, I grew used to this quite contained bilinguality. Gibraltarians speak English with a decided (or, rather, an undecided) accent — a slightly staccato English

altogether free of the characteristic Spanish s-stumblings —
yet at the same time their Spanish is not the famously lazy,
lisping Andalusian spoken across the frontier but a casual,
slurred Spanish of their own, incorporating many English
words, like *"tipol"* and *"sospán"* for "teapot" and "saucepan."
They suffer no ambiguity of mind, however, and straddle both
traditions quite jauntily, following the bullfights and filling
in their English football-pool coupons. The ambiguity exists
mostly in the eye of the beholder. I was told of an Englishwoman who, arriving in Gibraltar, stopped suddenly and remarked, "Oh, I say — your policemen dress just like *our* policemen!" The Gibraltarian who told me the story said he had
spent a long time trying to think of a way to clarify her mind,
but had finally given up, deciding that it would be simpler to
work wholeheartedly for Gibraltar's independence.

Present-day Gibraltarians have a bizarre racial background.
When the British took the Rock, in 1704, the resident Spaniards
were allowed to evacuate it peaceably, and they settled in the
nearby Spanish village of San Roque, where they continued to
regard themselves as the rightful inhabitants of Gibraltar. A
small settlement of Genoese, however, elected to remain in
Gibraltar under British rule, and later they were joined by
other Italians and by some of the Sephardim — the descendants
of the Jews of Spain, who had taken refuge in various parts of
the world — who came to trade and settle in Gibraltar by way
of Portugal and Leghorn. Since Queen Anne, in 1705, had declared Gibraltar a free port, the local population carried on a
lively trade with North Africa and with Spain, and new strains
gradually insinuated themselves into the native population; Portuguese settled in large numbers, members of the shifting British
garrison often elected to stay in Gibraltar, and eventually

Spaniards and Maltese and more Italians came and took root. The present population is a thorough fusion of these mainly Mediterranean elements, and is predominantly Roman Catholic; the Jews, however, have adhered to their faith, and have had a profoundly important influence on the well-being of the colony.

Gibraltar really has two quite separate histories: the small, private history of its native inhabitants (the noun "native" is frowned on, probably because it has always been used rather indiscriminately by the British), and its long, more spectacular history as a fortress that has never lost any of its importance through a succession of European wars — an importance that even now, for all the shift in strategic emphasis, has not in the least diminished in the eyes of any of the bristling military types I spoke to. I spent a good part of my time in the Garrison Library — a graceful, well-kept building with a notice board cluttered with small, diffident announcements of phonograph recitals, country-dance-group teas, and committee meetings — looking through its impressive collection of works on Gibraltar. Eventually, I settled down with the 1777 edition of *A Journey from Gibraltar to Malaga, with a View of That Garrison and Its Environs,* by Francis Carter, Esq., F.S.A. His preface put me firmly in my place:

There have been hitherto no other accounts of this coast published in our language but the cursory remarks and vague descriptions of English gentlemen, who, making but a few days' residence at its capital towns, often only as many hours, could not be expected (how much merit soever they might otherwise possess) to give any regular history of a people with whose language they were wholly unacquainted: I have known Spain from my very childhood, since the year 1753, to 1773; all my time (except for five years spent in France) was passed in Andalusia and the kingdom of Granada; during so long an absence from my native country, I sought consolation through the study of that in which it was my lot to reside.

I decided to go respectfully on with Mr. Carter:

The Moors under Tarif-Abenzarca, in the year of Our Lord 714, were the first who noticed the natural strength of the place; they built, peopled, and fortified both the castle and town. . . . The hill lost its ancient name of Calpe on the arrival of Tarif, who called it after himself Gibel-Tarif, or Tarif's mountain; Abdulmalic, historian of the kings of Morocco, deduces its present name from Gibel-tath, or the Mountain of the Entrance, being the key that led them into Spain; but Leo Africanus says expressly its truest derivation is from Gibel-fetoh, which in Arabick signifies the Mountain of Victory, [and] Abulcacim Tarif Abentarique calls it by a similar name, Jabal-fath. Hence Gibraltar by the Spaniards.

Gibraltar was occupied and reoccupied several times in the wars between Moors and Spaniards before Spain settled down in possession of it, in 1462, and set about restoring its fortifications. When Queen Isabella of Spain died, in 1504, she commanded in her will that her heirs undertake the sacred charge of holding Gibraltar. It was she who awarded Gibraltar its coat of arms — a castle with a key pendent and an inscription that reads, "Seal of the Noble City of Gibraltar, the Key of Spain." In spite of her injunction, Gibraltar fell to a combined British and Dutch fleet in 1704, during the War of the Spanish Succession, and, over Dutch protests, the British dug themselves in, fending off a few abortive Spanish attempts to regain it until the Treaty of Utrecht, in 1713, left them in ratified possession. In a Gibraltar bar one night, I overheard an intricate argument over what was precisely implied in the wording of the treaty, which made it clear to me that loose prose, particularly in treaties, is not a thing to leave lying about.

Treaty or no treaty, the Spaniards seem never quite to have

given up hope of recovering the Peñón, as they call the Rock. Throughout most of the eighteenth century they besieged it with waspish repetition, but it was in 1779, during the Maritime Wars, in which Spain allied herself to France for the single purpose of recovering Gibraltar and Minorca, that the four-year-long Great Siege — the most dramatic single episode in Gibraltar's knobbled past — was launched. An enormous and excited Franco-Spanish Army entrenched itself on the isthmus facing the Rock, little more than a cannon shot away. As every American schoolboy knows, the British were greatly extended elsewhere at the time, and could not reliably be expected to sustain the garrison (which amounted to about five and a half thousand men) from the sea. Gibraltar's number appeared to be up.

I read several accounts of the Great Siege in the Library — even one in the faded handwritten original — and it was not difficult for me to imagine myself back to the circumstances of it, particularly since I had only to glance out of the window to verify places and distances. In the same way, both sides must have noted each other's every activity throughout the four years. The garrison had the good fortune to be commanded by General George Augustus Eliott, in every sense the right man to have on one's side. (In the Alameda Gardens there is a greening bust of him — beetle-browed, with a great hook nose — and a copy of a portrait of him by Reynolds hangs in the Gibraltar Museum.) All during the cruel deprivations of the siege — at one point, ammunition was so low that the batteries had to restrict themselves to firing three shots a day, which they referred to as the Father, the Son, and the Holy Ghost — Eliott maintained a roistering, good-humored discipline, and, beyond that, was able to show remarkable military ingenuity. In November, 1781, he had the audacity to launch a secret

[52]

night attack, using a third of his men, on the forward Spanish batteries, and completely destroyed them. (Sortie Day is still observed by the Army in Gibraltar.) Eliott also encouraged his men to think up schemes that might break the stalemate, and eventually gave his permission to one, Sergeant-Major Ince, to tunnel long galleries close to the surface of the Rock, at a height of six hundred feet, from which to fire down on the Spaniards. The galleries still exist, with some of the guns in position, pointing dizzily down at the present airstrip. It was an astonishing piece of engineering, considering the times and circumstances, and one that made a good deal more practical sense than the detailed plan with which a Spanish engineer approached the Duc de Crillon, the French commander, for building a vast mountain, higher than Gibraltar, a short way inland, "thus depriving the fortress of its chief advantage." Crillon declined to build the mountain, but he did put all his eggs into building ten floating batteries — huge, heavily armed hulls filled with damp sand and cork to prevent their catching fire. The British could watch them being readied across the bay, and as the climax of the siege drew near, thousands of spectators gathered on the surrounding hills to see Gibraltar fall. On the morning of September 13, 1782, the ten batteries lumbered to their stations, about a thousand yards from the shore. At his home in Sussex, prior to coming out to assume the Governorship, Eliott had with quiet aplomb practiced using heated cannon balls, and he now proceeded to rain red-hot fire on the batteries until, by afternoon, wispy flames began to show from the *Pastora,* the flagship of the attacking fleet. Crillon's supporting craft arrived too late, and by midnight most of the anchored ships were ablaze or had blown up. Spanish and French casualties numbered about two thousand, and Gibraltar was still intact. Crillon withdrew, and in the next month Lord Howe brilliantly manoeuvred a relieving fleet into the bay. The siege petered out the following February, and although the Peace of Versailles clipped back the British Empire and let Spain keep Minorca and Florida, Britain sat on Gibraltar, and Spain lost its last chance to negotiate for its restoration. On the Spanish and French side, the Great Siege was mismanaged, but this in no way dims the doggedness and audacity of the garrison. By the time I had read two or three accounts of the siege, and had noted General Eliott's elevation to the peerage, as Lord Heathfield, I might have cheered aloud had it not been for the presence of two formidable-looking ladies in the Library.

"If Jimmy gets a horse, he'll be absolutely all right," said the first.

"Yes, and since it *is* an English company . . ." said the other.

I replaced the heroic documents and left.

All British schoolboys, at some stage or other, are given a toy fort and a miscellany of tin soldiers, often handed down by a graduating generation, with which they acquire a tidy sense of nursery strategy, and something of this addiction has gone into Gibraltar's evolution as a fortress. It is so neatly ingenious. Burrowing in the wake of Sergeant-Major Ince, engineers ran rabbit-wild inside the Rock itself, and now there is an estimated thirty miles of tunnelling, concealing who knows what. (Characteristically, the loose excavated rock was used as the foundations for the reclaimed dock areas and for the seaward extension of the airstrip.) Since the place depends for its water supply mainly on rainfall, great catchments cover the higher and steeper slopes, the rain running into enormous reservoirs inside the Rock. Roads have been masterfully imagined, to give unlikely access to even the upper Rock —

tidy little roads, with a goodly lining of green shade. Bare though the Rock may look from the sea, its semi-tropical vegetation is surprisingly profuse and varied — pines, cypresses, and wild olives abound — and throughout the town there are, of course, multitudes of those small, parade-ground garden patches that British servicemen manage to conjure out of whatever wilderness they find themselves in.

The First World War and, more dramatically, the Second underlined the stupendous importance of Gibraltar as a military, naval, and air base; it virtually kept Britain afloat in the Mediterranean, especially during the period when the Axis controlled practically the entire Mediterranean coastline. I recall putting in to the Rock a few times during the war, when the immediate vicinity was aboil, and finding it a brisk beehive of military efficiency — so much so that in the end we scarcely bothered to go ashore, for life in the fortress was even tenser and more controlled than it was on shipboard. Gibraltar's very existence at that point was like a blow struck. Whenever we spotted the great doubled fist of the Rock from seaward, it always cheered us up. On this occasion, the second morning I was there I watched three destroyers slip from the harbor, with much booping of sirens, and turn in line into the bay. I must say they looked stirring to me. It is the efficient compactness of everything — dockyard, harbor, airfield, fortifications, roads, barracks, hospitals — that gives the place its air of intense, concentrated importance, like a clockwork microcosm. Since, as my friend Francis Carter remarks, "the English being a nation that, in all their colonies spread over the face of the globe, study more the useful than the grand," and since Gibraltar still has its thumb on the approaches to the Mediterranean and its eye cocked toward Spain and Africa, there seems little likelihood that Britain will ever seriously consider giving it back to anyone. Even to the small gray pillow of cloud that, by repute, hangs perpetually over the forehead of the Rock, Gibraltar is stiff with Englishness, with that ripe, determined cheer and relentless go that the English emanate. When something has to be done or solved, however unpleasant, the English take a rare, secret pleasure in getting on with it; it is when there is no particular task or hardship in sight that they falter. Unlike the Spaniards, they have little natural talent for being alone, although they suffer their boredom dauntlessly. On Main Street, I noticed Spaniards eyeing pretty women with their habitual delighted Mediterranean wonder; the British servicemen, on the other hand, looked at them with quiet, furtive desperation, as they might have eyed forbidden candy. In the Alameda Gardens, I played on a fiendishly contrived miniature golf course, full of traps and obstacles, which seemed to represent, *in parvo*, the ferocious ingenuity of the whole place, and as I came away I passed a sign that read:

> These gardens are cultivated for your pleasure.
> Please coöperate by observing these rules:
> 1. Do not touch the plants or walk on the flower beds.
> 2. Keep dogs on a leash while in the garden.
> 3. Do not leave litter in the garden.

Below, the same text followed in Spanish, but the Spanish read as if it had been unwillingly dragged there, like a child forcibly dressed up for an occasion. All through the town, there is a tyranny of well-groomed signs. Every eventuality has been provided for in advance, every small aspect of the place accounted for. I read my way through no less than five volumes of statistics on the colony, and could not help marvelling at their minuteness. Perhaps this is why Gibraltar has no *mystique*; it has all been patiently organized down to the last detail. Even the resident ape population has an officer in charge of it. The colony has an impressive array of social services, and pays scrupulous attention to itself.

Relations between Gibraltarians and British, however, have not always been quite as amiable as they now appear to be. In the past, Gibraltar suffered from what is officially called a "fortress mentality"; Gibraltarians complained that military considerations were apt to take precedence over the well-being of the community, and the pointed aloofness of the British tended to put the local inhabitants on edge. It is not difficult to understand this ruffling of feelings. The British govern their colonies gently but firmly, as a nanny might ("Yes, dear, but Britain knows best"), with a kind of instinctive gamesmanship — a tacit underlying assumption of superiority that provokes a slow, shuffling resentment, although on the surface their rule is so cool, so efficient, so fair and just that one must always seriously admire it on paper and in retrospect. Now, however, the edginess has all but gone. In 1950, by Royal Instructions, a Legislative Council was created, presided over by the Governor and consisting of twelve members — three civil-service officials, two members nominated by the Governor, and seven elected members (a majority), all seven of whom are Gibraltarians. This naturally gave Gibraltarians a substantial measure of control over their own affairs, and has been taken extremely seriously by the local population; the British colonial officials, too, have been forced to concern themselves more minutely and less blandly with Gibraltar's internal affairs. Two or three times during my stay, I found myself in the midst of colony-shaking arguments — arguments that seemed to be a part of a regular, running conversation. They generally arose over some small local matter currently preoccupying the Legislative Council and almost always led into large speculations on the future of the colony, since the Gibraltarians, having now got a grip on their own destiny, feel the day to be at hand when they will have to choose — or at least approach Nanny with the question — whether they will have complete self-determination. Even though they have fought energetically for their present representation, they remain sharply divided over what they want next. From all the argument, I gathered that Gibraltarians are very proud of the steps they have taken toward governing themselves, and that their speculations on the future are a kind of muscle-flexing — a rather abrupt extension of their new-found sense of responsibility. The chances are that they will gain almost complete control over internal affairs in the colony, at the same time leaving the British pretty much in charge of the place *qua* fortress. Local happenings are national issues — Gibraltar has all the problems of being a full colony with no more resources than those of a small town.

Gibraltarians are serious people, and they are also awesomely industrious. Several times I met the mayor of Gibraltar, Mr. J. A. Hassan, C.B.E., M.V.O., J.P., as he darted in and out of other people's offices, but I was never able to corner him until one sunny afternoon when he picked me up on the road and drove me into the town. A small, high-voiced man with a wiry, intense intelligence, he talked eagerly and excitedly to me as we sat in his car outside the freshly painted Town Hall.

"You've probably been trying to puzzle us out and put us in pigeonholes," he said, with a sudden, charming smile. "Well, I'm glad to tell you that we won't fit, either as Spaniards or as Englishmen. We have learned enormously from the British in that we follow the rules — we respect punctuality and efficiency, we keep our word, and we believe in fair play, the law, and an ordered way of life. Spaniards find us puzzling. For instance, I was talking recently to a Spanish officer, and he said to me, 'Look, Hassan, you've been mayor now for the last twelve years — you must be doing well for yourself.' The truth is that I have been so absorbed in civic affairs and in constitutional reform, which is my preoccupation, that I have had scarcely any time for my law practice, and, as you know, we receive only a token salary for our administrative duties. The officer was horrified when I told him. We like to think that we embody the best elements of our dual temperament. Our elections are orderly and fair, and we would not think of corrupting them. At the same time, we do feel ourselves to be Latin in the sense that the positions we take are never purely theoretical ones — we shift and adjust them until they fit our particular situations, bearing individuals in mind. Gibraltar politics are *human* politics, not in the least theoretical. I would call myself a Socialist in economics and a liberal in politics, yet you may hear me occasionally referred to as a right-wing capitalist. Actually, the definitions need scarcely ever arise here; the place is small enough to allow us to act *particularly,* in terms of what we immediately want to achieve, for the general good. I have lost count of the number of committees I sit on, but we get our business done because we are all so continuously in touch with one another." So saying, he darted quickly out of the car.

Later, I spoke to him in his office overlooking John Mackintosh Square, and again I got the impression that even if plans and decisions on the future of the colony did not yet exist on paper, they were already humming about in the mayor's head. "We have all had to learn the art of compromise from the British," he told me. "But I think that we have also taught them many things, and have made them grow a little more human in their application of principle. As you probably realize, we have been trying our wings for the last ten years, and we fly, on the whole, pretty well."

Gibraltar's Main Street has a surprising habit of filling up and emptying quite suddenly; cruise ships arrive and land their passengers for a two-hour jaunt through the bulging shops, and as quickly spirit them away. (It is quite astonishing how many people turn out to have either landed at or touched at Gibraltar. In 1878, General U. S. Grant was given a banquet in St. George's Hall, the chamber that Sergeant-Major Ince hollowed out of the rock, and in 1919 the Abbé Henri Breuil discovered, in the course of a walk, the site of a shelter of the Mousterian period, about 40,000 B.C., at the base of the Rock on the north front.) Tourists are so important to Gibraltar's economy that shopkeepers enjoy a special dispensation to open on Sundays should a ship dock. The limited duty that, thanks to Queen Anne, makes almost everything cheaper in Gibraltar keeps its streets well trodden and its cash registers ringing, but Gibraltarians seem thoroughly bored with their own plenty. You cannot, after all, buy a watch or a high-power telescope all that often, nor can you go on gazing like a hungry sailor into windows draped with satin cushion covers and brimming over with papier-mâché models of the Rock that play "Annie Laurie." Nevertheless, tourism looms large in Gibraltar's future, and the foundations are already laid for two vast new hotels, even for a casino. It is, however, difficult to imagine how the Rock can, like some genial Gulliver, bear any more human traffic. The prosperity of the place has already caused every local inhabitant who can afford one to get himself a gleaming new car, with the comic result that there are more cars in ratio to the population in Gibraltar than practically anywhere else in the world. The consequences, though, are far from comic, since it is constantly necessary to press oneself flat against the walls of the already narrow streets to avoid being run down. Moreover, there is scarcely anywhere for cars to go except into the Rock itself. "Yesterday, I drove my car the quarter of a mile from my house to the office," one official told me, "and then, after I had crawled about for half an hour looking for a parking place, I had to drive back home, only to find that the space outside my house had been filled. I was an hour late for work." The steps to be taken are so obvious that it is only a matter of time until cars are eliminated from the town, yet the people have grown so to look forward to their weekend jaunts into Spain that their cars have become for them symbols not only of prosperity but of escape from the cramped confinement of the place.

Relations between Spain and Gibraltar, like those between Britain and Gibraltar, have not always been as temperate as they now are; in fact, it is only in the past two years that they have returned to being at all easy. As recently as 1956, General Franco, drawing himself up to his full height of five feet four inches, declared in a rare press interview that the return of Gibraltar to Spain was a matter of honor for every Spaniard, adding that "the present state of Gibraltar is contrary to the whole spirit of postwar Europe" — a typically bizarre statement, considering the present state of Spain. In 1954, the year marking the two-hundred-and-fiftieth anniversary of the British seizure of the Rock, Franco gave vent to a savage burst of propaganda and invective against the proposed visit of the Queen in that year to Gibraltar, and he managed to whip up a great deal of agitation at the time, perhaps because he felt then that he had the United States on his side, but more likely because he has always smarted under the slighting treatment he has had at the hands of the British. At any rate, the British

Embassy in Madrid was stoned and mobbed, and the Queen's life was actually threatened by letter. Franco also referred obliquely to a secret agreement allegedly made by Churchill during the Second World War, by which Spain would receive Gibraltar in return for staying neutral. But the British did not budge, and the Queen made her visit in peace. Franco's rampage subsided in the following year, but not before he had closed the Spanish consulate in Gibraltar, barred Spanish tourists from visiting the Rock, and provoked a flurry of measures and countermeasures that made the crossing of the frontier, for both Spaniards and Gibraltar residents, corrosively difficult. Most of my Spanish friends conceded that "the Gibraltar question" was nothing more than a convenient escape valve for the General, through which he expressed his more sinister irritations; in any case, not one of the Spanish workers with whom I spoke in cafés on both sides of the frontier considered the return of Gibraltar anything short of a disastrous prospect. "It's not a matter of honor in *my* soul," said one cheerful little waiter. "It's a matter of daily bread — or, let's say, daily cigarettes. I'd like to see Franco feed us just once the way we eat off Gibraltar." Since Franco has subsequently become much more of a beggar than a chooser, the animosity has subsided, and Gibraltarians are again able to take their pleasure in Spain. "Lot of fuss about nothing," growled one Army major when we discussed it. "There's only one thing that Franco can do about Gibraltar, and that's to saw it off."

When the time came to leave Gibraltar, I decided to walk to La Línea and take a bus along the coast of Málaga, more or less following the route of my mentor Mr. Carter. The morning was sunny, and so still that the sound of hammering, and even of voices, floated up from the dockyard. In front of the

Governor's Residence, the guard was changing itself again, with a crunch of boots and a tight punctuation of commands. I stopped to read one last notice, which in itself was a monument to the place:

THE PUBLIC ARE WARNED THAT UNDER THE PROVISIONS OF PARA-GRAPH (35) OF SECTION 3 OF THE SUMMARY CONVICTION ORDINANCE IT IS AN OFFENCE TO ENCOURAGE THE ROCK APES TO COME DOWN FROM THE UPPER ROCK OR TO FEED THEM AT ANY PLACE OTHER THAN THE QUEEN'S GATE ROAD, BETWEEN THE AERIAL STANDARD AND THE QUEEN'S GATE, OR AT QUEEN'S GATE, AND ANY PERSON CON-VICTED OF SUCH AN OFFENCE SHALL BE LIABLE TO A PENALTY NOT EXCEEDING £10.

In Gibraltar town, shops were beginning to open up, and barrowloads of flowers stood in the main square. As one walks toward Spain, the town actually grows more Spanish — the cafés are dingier and smaller, and a crowd of women buzzes about the open fish market. I began to meet the steady stream of workers tramping in for their day's work, lunch in hand and brown, creased faces squinting in the sun. As I left the town and started to cross the width of the airstrip, I already felt Gibraltar beginning to recede and loom. Looking up at the rock face, I could just distinguish the small dotted line of Ince's gunports across it, and I felt that, from some small look-out on its woody forehead, an ape might possibly be watching me go. To reach the Spanish frontier, one has to cross the Neutral Ground, a windswept expanse of scrub, smelling of the sea, with occasional concrete pillboxes dotted about. At the gate on the British side, two blue-uniformed policemen saluted briskly, glanced at my passport, and, addressing me by name, wished me a good morning and passed me through to the Spanish policemen on the other side. These leafed their way slowly through the passport, peering at it page by page. It was all very formal. How long was I to be in Spain? I replied that I lived in Spain. Oh? Then what was I doing in Gibraltar? I had been visiting Gibraltar. Oh. The faces of the Spanish policemen had not mastered the impassivity of their British counterparts. They changed quickly from suspicion to puzzlement to curiosity to wonder. I could go now.

At the other end of the Neutral Ground, I walked through an arch, past an indifferent customs official who was picking his nails, and came into the main plaza of La Línea. The transition was comically sudden. Rickety café tables and chairs sprawled across the sidewalks and into the road. The white walls were blinding in the sun. Dogs lay snoring in the gutters. Children were splashing water over one another from a fountain, spraying it into the air in great, glistening arcs. Men lounged about in twos and threes, talking and gesticulating. Women with bulging vegetable baskets called out, laughed, and scolded. It was hard even to think myself back across the odd half-mile into Gibraltar. There everything had been so polite and brisk and private; here the life of the place was spilling out of the houses into the street — old clothes and slippers replaced the neatness of uniforms. I pushed my way past two donkeys into the cool dark interior of a café on the heels of a fat little Spaniard who had waddled across the frontier in front of me and who was greeted jovially by the two or three men sitting over dominoes at a zinc table close to the bar. They had begun to talk excitedly when one of the men jerked his head in my direction, and they all stopped and looked at me. The waiter came forward. What did I want? I replied that I wanted a glass of beer, and could he tell me where I could catch the bus for Málaga? The bus would be outside in the plaza in about twenty minutes' time, he told me, but I would not be able to get back to Gibraltar tonight. It did not matter, I said, since I had only been visiting the place. Officially? No, I was only curious to see what it was like, and what went on there. The men began to laugh, and the small, fat one came up to me. "The Señor has come at a good moment," he said, and winked. "We can show him what goes on, all right, and how amiable we feel toward the Peñón. Although Spain is our mother, Gibraltar, you must understand, is our aunt, and, as it happens in human life, aunts are always kinder to us children than mothers are."

As he spoke, he was undoing his belt, and, pulling on a string that was fastened to it, he reverently drew a bottle of whiskey from the recesses of his trouser leg. "A gift from the Queen of England to the disloyal subjects of General Franco!" he shouted, thumping it proudly on the bar.

The others cackled, and he wormed a bottle of English gin from his other trouser-leg. "A gift from the Governor of Gibraltar to Lucho Montesinos! May he keep on his profitable fat feet these many years!"

While I drank my beer, he unpinned two cartons of cigarettes and a variety of small articles from the lining of his jacket and piled them up beside the bottles. "Now, Señor," he said to me, "I am going to uncork this glorious whiskey, and, early in the day though it is, we will drink a toast together to Aunt Gibraltar, who is so kind to us, and whom may God reward with many years of life. If ever it should be ours again, we will tidy it up and present it once more to the great Queen Isabel, who is so gracious. Is she not?"

The others nodded and smiled. We drank.

Euzkadi — 1961

THE chances of encountering one's double in this life must be fairly slim. Nevertheless, I have begun to believe that even the most oddly shaped of us has a double — unsuspected and unsuspecting, working away quietly in some unlikely context — for I had the curious experience not of meeting mine but of passing an impressionable night and day in his natural habitat, in the Basque province of Vizcaya, on the northern coast of Spain. My double is a Basque sea captain who lives, between voyages, on the fringes of the town of Guernica, and I have made a tentative promise to return there when he gets back from his current voyage. I doubt if I shall go. If we confront one another, the differences between us will become obvious; as it was, in his absence, his friends all swore to our absolute duplication of one another, with much exclamation and headshaking.

I made the pilgrimage to Guernica for a concentration of reasons, after travelling about in the Basque country, from village to village, between the mountains and the sea. The name reverberates familiarly mainly through the agency of Picasso's painting, but Picasso was only underlining the infamy of the town's complete annihilation by German bombers during the Spanish Civil War — an act of such ruthless vindictiveness that the mere mention of the name still stops conversations in Spain. But beyond that, Guernica has a much greater importance — an importance, in fact, that led to its being selected for annihilation. It was and is the symbolic capital of the Basque race, the old seat of government, where oaths were taken and laws made under its venerable oak tree, the Tree of Guernica. Here, traditionally, the elder Basque statesmen met on all matters concerning the land that Basques call Euzkadi — a mythical entity that now exists more vividly in my awareness than do many more politically established countries.

There are four Basque provinces in the north of Spain — Vizcaya, Guipúzcoa, Alava, and Navarra — which extend along the Bay of Biscay to the French border, and which, together with the three French districts of Soule, Labourde, and Basse-Navarre, form the seven provinces of Euzkadi. Although politically the Basques are Spaniards or Frenchmen (or Argentines, Venezuelans, Americans, or Australians, since they emigrate readily and always with distinction), Euzkadi is the country they continue to inhabit in the back of their minds; and while they fulfill the formalities of what they regard as their second citizenship with energy and responsibility, they look on themselves first as Basques. The respect with which they are universally regarded is a respect for those qualities of responsibility and independence, which are ruggedly Basque and which resist without difficulty all varieties of national influence.

Guernica sits squarely in a broad green valley on the river Mundaca, and to get to it I had to catch a miniature train that connected with the main line between Bilbao and San Sebastián. The train, flying through the green fields, was full of chickens in hampers and chattering passengers who waved to solitary figures working in the landscape and called to them by name. I had no ticket for this stage of the journey, which perplexed the conductor. I would have to pay six pesetas, which was fifty centimos more than if I had bought my ticket beforehand. It hurt him. Borrowing a pencil from me, he wrote out a long, patient receipt. Had I been before in Guernica? No, never, but I wanted both to visit the Tree and to see how the town had been rebuilt. Then I knew about the happenings? Yes, I did. He shook his head for a long time. I would be staying in Guernica at least overnight? Yes, indeed. He wagged his finger, and went off to talk with an old man at the other end of the car, jerking his head from time to time in my direction. When he came back, he handed me a paper. This was the name of the inn where I would be most comfortable, and this was the café where I would meet the old ones of the town, those who had been there *before;* here was the proprietor's name, and here was the name of someone who would show me the Tree and the archives. I thanked him, and he apologized that he could not be there himself. The train drew in to Guernica, and he shook my hand and went off, my pencil still behind his ear.

At Guernica, the train practically emptied. Most of the people were being met — but then Spaniards scarcely ever undertake journeys of any kind without being seen off or welcomed by throngs of relatives and children. The air in Spanish airports and railroad stations throbs steadily with emotion. I took my bag and walked through the town, which had the square, cemented anonymity of all new buildings in Spain, serving their purpose but no more, unworn, unfinished, built out of an uninspired necessity but with no affection. Spain gives the impression of having been dragged unwillingly into the technological age; its heart is not there. Instead, sullenly resentful of modernity, it contrives successfully to make all instances of it seem cold, drab, and forlorn.

I found room at the inn without any difficulty — tourists in Guernica, I discovered, are mainly expatriate Basques who come in high summer to visit the Tree — and eventually made my way to the café suggested by the conductor. Conversation stopped as I entered, and the small knots of men at the bar looked at me cautiously. I nodded to them, and addressed the landlord, who surprised me by speaking English — he had gone to school in England, he told me, while his father, a Basque, was first mate with an English shipping line. As time passed, I began to be aware that the men in the bar were still talking about me, but since they were speaking in the sharp, swift cadence of Basque, I could gather nothing of what they said. Just then, two other men entered, and one of them, catching sight of me, came over, thumped me on the shoulders, and welcomed me back with great enthusiasm. I told him that he must be mistaking me for someone else, since I had never before been in Guernica. His face stiffened in astonishment, and at that point four or five of the other men in the bar came across quickly and surrounded us, all talking at once. One of them took me aside to explain in Spanish.

"You must forgive us our rudeness in staring at you," he said, "but the truth is you resemble exactly a man who lives in this valley — but exactly! — and when you came in we all believed you to be him, except for the fact that you are not wearing a beret and are not dressed as he would be. He is captain of a ship out of Pasajes, and we expect him home any time now. We cannot get over the likeness."

The others pressed forward to assure me that I was in every respect the double of the captain, who was called Lorenzo. I must be Basque? No. Then of Basque ancestry? I did not think so. One of the men, short, thick-shouldered, and merry-eyed, asked if I would mind helping him win a bet, to prove how absolute was the resemblance. I concurred, and he asked me to sit on a particular stool facing the door, and to remove my tie and put on his beret. A farmer from down the valley, a cousin of Lorenzo's, was due in the bar at any moment, and my friend had laid a wager with the landlord that the farmer would take me for Lorenzo within a minute of entering the café now that I was properly dressed.

I had barely sat myself down, bereted and tieless, when the door creaked open and two men came in, blinking in the light. The taller of the two looked around the bar, nodding here and there; then, catching sight of me, he started suddenly. "Lorenzo!" he called out. "But you are back too soon!"

Everyone in the bar roared, and the short man rushed over to explain the wager to him. I took off the beret and put on my tie. Wryly, the landlord lined the bar with wineglasses. By now, the conversation was all conjecture over the ultimate encounter between Lorenzo and myself, which I agreed would have to take place. We were all in a high good humor.

The Basques are anything but taciturn, but while they cut swathes of talk around any subject at all — playfully, without ever seeming to take a sharp point of view — their convictions, I have found, are deep and firm, always lying under the surface and remaining for the most part unspoken. Humor runs away with them wildly. Their conversations are full of glee — extravagant exercises in preposterousness. At bottom, they are the proudest and most serious people in the world, yet they are constantly making fun of their own pride. I listened one evening in Saint-Jean-de-Luz to a long straight-faced discourse proving that the mother of Yuri Gagarin was a Basque; the man who advanced the claim did so with such vehemence that he all but convinced himself, I felt. To the Basques, being born a Basque is nothing short of a miracle, yet at the same time they are free from the steady self-preoccupation that marks other small, more uncertain minor races.

That evening in Guernica became a cascade of talk, once my companions got over the impulse to goggle at me and referred to me simply as "Lorenzo." Most of the company were farmers or seafaring men, natives of Guernica, yet in one another's company the subject of the past scarcely ever came up. They had no particular reluctance to talk about it, and did so with me in the most matter-of-fact way; but among themselves it was emphatically over and gone.

"Don't forget how it is with us Basques," one of them said. "We were here in our small corner of Europe before anyone else, and we're still holding on to the same bit of country — no bigger, no smaller — that we had then. By the accident of time, we're counted as Spaniards, but we still work and live here in our own way; the more they plague us from the outside, the more Basque we become."

At that moment, two newcomers entered the café, and I noticed that the company switched from Spanish, which they had been speaking for my benefit, to Basque. The two men drank uncomfortably and left quickly. "Foreigners!" growled the short man. "After the Civil War, when we were rebuilding Guernica — with no help from the government — Franco thought he would water us down by shipping a lot of Andalusians up here.

[71]

He should have known better — that in our own country we don't mix. He might as well have sent us Eskimos."

Guernica was destroyed on the afternoon of April 26, 1937, after the Spanish Civil War had been raging for eleven months, and nothing that General Franco did in the course of the whole war caused such universal waves of horror and alarm. At that time in history, the Basques had newly gained their independence, for which they had been pressing strongly during the dictatorship of Primo de Rivera and the years of the Spanish Republic. Progress had been slow, since first Primo de Rivera and later the Republicans were loath to give way to separatist groups, their main aim being to draw Spain together. When the Civil War did break out, however, the Republicans, to make sure of the support of the Basques, granted them autonomy, and in October, 1936, the first president of the new Basque Republic, José Antonio de Aguirre, was sworn in under the Tree of Guernica. The fighting in the Basque provinces was markedly bitter; the accounts of the bombing of Guernica that I heard that evening, however, were, if anything, laconic — the memory was clear enough, but the strong feeling was suppressed and the vision cold.

"I had gone that afternoon up the valley to Amorebeita to ask my uncle, who lives there to this day, if he could lay hands on a sack or two of ground meal for me, for at that time we were just beginning to feel the food shortage," one man said. "As I was saying good-bye to him, we saw a plane with Nationalist markings circling slowly over the valley, but we thought little of it — stray planes often used to pass over to take a look at us. But as I was riding my bicycle back to Guernica, the bombers began to overtake me, flying very low. I heard some explosions, but could not believe they had anything to do with

[72]

us, until I caught sight of flames in the distance. It was a Monday afternoon, and Monday, by tradition, is our market day; many people had come in to town from round about, and had gone, as usual, to the *frontón* to watch a game of pelota. From behind me the planes kept coming and coming, and I could make out not only the German markings but the men in the cockpits. They drove into Guernica like buses, and by the time I reached the edge of town, pedalling furiously, the whole center was on fire from the showers of incendiary bombs they dropped. I left my bicycle and climbed the hill above our house, which already I could see was half-burned. On the way, I ran into my wife and two children, with a group of people who had left home at the first sign of the bombing. We knew nothing of what was happening, or why; there was little we could do but watch. I sent my wife and children to my cousin's house, across the valley. A group of us stayed, almost in a trance, scarcely feeling. The bombardment lasted barely three hours, but Guernica burned all night and well into the next day. I went at evening to see that my family was all right and then came back, to watch and wait. Most of those who escaped made their way either to Bilbao or to the houses of friends and neighbors in the countryside. There were a few of us who waited for the fires to go down, saying nothing. Next day, we went back into what was left of the town. Five buildings still stood; the Tree was unharmed. I found a cellar, which I occupied for a time with four others. We got together some supplies and began to work on the ruins, with shovels. Bit by bit, the people came back, and now, twenty-four years later, we have a new town. We built it ourselves, to wipe out that one day from our memory, and I suppose that if you question us now, all we will say is that the new town is more comfortable than the old one was. Once, I thought I would never forget all that, but now I find it is no more than a happening in the memory."

Later, when I left the café, I walked through the moonlit town with the cousin of my double. As we passed various buildings, he would pat an occasional buttress or wall and say, "These stones were there before; I remember building on top of them," or "That house there did not burn" — as though he carried in his head a complete map of the place as it once was, stone by stone.

The next morning the short, bright-eyed man — whose name, I had discovered, was the name on my piece of paper — called early to take me to the Tree. Together, we climbed a broad flight of steps to the chapel at the top of the town, which contains a small, crowded library of writings on the Basques. The original oak tree had been retired in 1860, he explained, after it had attained its legendary thousand years; its trunk is preserved there in a kind of Greek portico. We walked out into the sunlit courtyard to inspect its successor, a healthy young tree of a hundred and one, and my companion removed his beret. "We used to have trouble with tourists who wanted a leaf or piece of bark from the Tree — Basques who came back from abroad. As it is, there is a flourishing descendant of the old tree in Buenos Aires, but in autumn I generally collect a few of the fallen leaves and send them to our people abroad." We sat down on a stone bench in the sun while the little man regaled me with some of the endless mass of history and legend concerning the Basques and which, later, in the library, I began to explore for myself.

"Don't worry too much about facts," he said to me as he left me in the reading room. "There are hardly any facts about us. We say that, like a good woman, we have no history. We're as old as the Pyrenees, and we're likely to last as long, without changing very much. That's all there is to it."

I became increasingly thankful for that piece of counsel as I read my way into the morass of writings that have accumulated around the mystery of the Basques. There is little question in anyone's mind but that they are the oldest surviving race in Europe, and were in all likelihood comfortably settled in their corner before the barbarian invasions; yet they have no ascertainable history — not, at least, until the twelfth century, and even then contemporary historians complained about the haze that obscured their origins. The Basque language provides the most tangible evidence of their oddness; structurally very curious, it has no firm similarity to any other existing language, and has been the main basis for the wilder suppositions that have been made about the Basques. Life in the Basque provinces, whether on the inland farms or in the fishing villages, has changed very little with time and still has a muscular, handmade tang; the songs, the tempestuous folk dances, the games, and the myths keep cropping up in spontaneous joy, with nothing of the aura of the museum. For all these reasons, ethnologists and philologists and mythologists and anthropologists have descended, and still descend, on the Basques with whoops of astonished delight, and go quickly to work hacking, chiselling, and surmising. By now, I have read so many improbable hypotheses on the origins and affinities of the Basque race that I have grown quite prepared to accept some of the more fanciful explanations, which, characteristically, are preferred by the Basques themselves. In an eighteenth-century pamphlet, the Abbé Lahetjuzan took pains to derive all the names in the Book of Genesis from Basque roots; the name of Eve, he explained, came from *"ezbai,"* a conjunction of the

Basque words *"ez,"* meaning "no," and *"bia,"* meaning "yes," and standing for the dual nature of all women.

The question that divides scholars is whether the Basques are in fact Iberians or whether they are directly descended from a paleolithic race that inhabited the Pyrenees before the Iberians arrived. From what I could glean with any certainty out of the violent pro-and-con, they are now allowed to be descended from a prehistoric Pyrenean race, but one modified and influenced by the Iberian invasions. Scholarly argument bases itself mostly on the discovery of ingenious linguistic parallels; freed from the onus of facts, the scholars have ranged about with abandon and, more recently, have taken to linking the Basque language with Caucasus mountain dialects — a thesis that has a higher degree of probability than some of their earlier venturings.

Characteristically, the Basques remain utterly unperturbed by the mystery of their origins; on the contrary, they are delighted by their own inexplicability. One Sunday afternoon in San Sebastián, I went with a Basque friend to the *frontón* to watch a game of *chistera* — pelota played with long, banana-shaped baskets. The game was magnificently exciting, the betting raucous, the spectators exuberant.

During the intermission, we ran into a local doctor at the bar. "If you are mistaken enough to be interested," he said to me, "I have in the house a learned treatise written by a German folklorist on the forms and variations of pelota, or handball, or whatever you want to call it proving it to be the oldest known game and full of strange implications that no Basque has ever dreamed of. This German came to see me once, but we did not get very far. He kept pressing me to tell him what I thought the game *meant,* and I told him it didn't mean anything at all; it simply *was.* Around here, as soon as we can walk, we begin to hit a ball against a wall, just for the pleasure of it, and it seems to me a singularly uncomplicated fact that we have been doing so for hundreds of years. Pleasure does not alter very much, and when we get old and short of breath, we come to the *frontón* to watch others do it better. I honestly fail to see the point of his treatise — it's of no interest to us Basques, whereas the game itself is. I took him to a game or two, but he never enjoyed a single moment; instead, he kept asking me questions about the height of the wall and the shape of the *chistera* — things like that. The game is just as old as the first ball, I told him. You may have the book, if you want it. I'm afraid it would only spoil my pleasure."

We all sat down together as the game began again, my friend and the doctor betting furiously against one another, catching the cutaway tennis balls that the bookies tossed up to them and extracting the red and blue betting slips stuffed inside.

"I'll tell you one thing, though," said the doctor, leaning across to me. "The *chistera* you see the players using came about quite by accident, when someone used a fruit basket to play pelota with. Now, in the souvenir shops, you can buy *chisteras* to use once again as fruit baskets. Everything, you see, straightens out with the passing of time. I wish I had remembered to tell that to the German."

While the Basque country forms a small, neat geographical unit fitting tidily into the right angle of the Bay of Biscay, it is no longer quite the entity it was, and the old Basque war cry "*Zazpiak Bat!*" ("The Seven Are One!") is something of an anachronism. In the past, when France and Spain happened to be at war, the seven Basque provinces bound themselves by *traités de bonne correspondance* to remain neutral; in the course of this century, however, the diverging political paths of France and Spain have split Euzkadi in two. The unity does survive in a purely local sense; the fishermen of the Spanish Basque coast have the same preoccupations as the fishermen of the French Basque coast, and they meet and talk together as Basques, although the Frenchmen may know no Spanish and the Spaniards no French. The Basque dialects vary slightly, but the fishing remains much the same. "We Basques have two selves," one fisherman in Saint-Jean-de-Luz put it. "If you ask us suddenly what we are, we will naturally reply that we are Basques. But, over and above that, we are Frenchmen, and we have fought as Frenchmen in two wars; in a moment we can become Frenchmen, pure and simple, like slipping on another coat. It's more difficult for the Spanish Basques. While France has been a kindly mother to us, Spain has been a cruel step-mother to them, and as a result they are more belligerently Basque than we want to be. For us, there is no contradiction; we're quite happy to think of ourselves as Frenchmen."

The differences, however, go much further than that. To reach the Basque country from southern Spain, one travels north across the endless spreading plains of Castile, parched in summer, slow and indolent, without a sign of water or life. After them, the small, green, humped hills and, eventually, the craggy, moist Atlantic coast are a relief — the frequent *chirimiri*, the light Basque rain, falls like a benison; the towns have a good-humored bustle about them; the people are inquisitive, active, decisive, and they mean business. But to make the brief journey across the frontier, at Irún, into France, although it amounts to going farther north geographically, is in fact to cross over into the laconic, easy-going air of the French Midi, where the day unwinds at a markedly slower pace under a hot, restraining sun, where work keeps stopping and starting, where

the berets flop limply over the eyes. The French Basque provinces are very much of the south, and take their pulse from
that, far more than from the exuberance of the Basque temperament. For this reason, they appear more theatrically Basque,
and the decorative side of Basque life — the fêtes and folk
dances, the pageants, the *pastorales*, the folk singing — is staged
more self-consciously in the French villages. The same things
happen in Spain, but in the natural context of Basque life. As
might also be expected, it is in France that one comes across the
souvenir shops, the thirsty Basque-hunting tourists, and anoma-
lies like Le Motel Basque, no less horrifying for their inevitability. The old whaling ports of Saint-Jean-de-Luz and Biarritz
have taken on new, luxurious, well-tailored identities, although
the fishermen still fish; prosperity has dulled the sharp edge. I
was chiding a French Basque for this one day when he stopped
me short. "Don't be altogether deceived by all the parapherna-
lia," he said. "You'll see plenty of prosperity now on both sides
of the border, and you'll probably conclude that it comes from
our success at selling Basque matchboxes to the tourists. That's
not all of it, by any means. Remember, for us Basques there is
no border — France and Spain put it up comparatively recently,
in the seventeenth century, and so gave us a new profession.
Basque free trade, we call it. Why shouldn't our Spanish kin
have some of the things we enjoy in France, and why shouldn't
we have an occasional taste of what they have? We're all
Basques, aren't we? Mutual benefit, that's what it is. We've
always claimed the right to move freely across the frontier, and
if it requires any ingenuity for us to take our luggage along,
too — well, we have plenty."

The Basques smuggle not only with ingenuity but, more,
with gusto, although I would consider it immoral to go into
detail. Enough to say that among the frontier Basques smug-

gling is practiced with an intense devotion that makes it almost rank with the two classic activities of Basques — sheepherding and seafaring. Basques believe quite confidently that they discovered America long before Columbus but came home again to Euzkadi, not bothering to mention the discovery; at any rate, their temperament has always taken easily and naturally to the sea. They were the first fishermen who dared to put out after whales in longboats, along the Biscay coast; watchtowers still punctuate the headlands. In the eighteenth century, inclined, as usual, to be on no one's side but their own, they took lucratively to piracy, and made handsome reputations as corsairs. Predictably, however, they came home with their spoils to the Basque country, married Basque girls, and settled in their native villages. Even though the coastal fishermen complain about the steady decline of the fishing, Basque seamen are still as indigenous to the sea lanes of the world as are Scottish engineers. A truck driver who gave me a lift one day told me that he signs on with a Norwegian line for a six-month voyage every two or three years, whenever he wants to buy a new truck.

As for sheepherding, the Basques are so renowned for that solitary occupation that they are nowadays in great demand, particularly in the sheep-raising regions of the United States. An average of about two hundred "alien sheepherders," as the Immigration Service has it, cross annually for a three-year stint. (They share the privilege with a rash of Basque pelota players, who spend the winter jai-alai season in Florida.) Most of the sheepherders return to the Basque country, generally with the scantiest knowledge of English, unperturbed by the experience. Sheep, after all, are sheep the world over.

In our present climate of incipient internationalism, with new countries taking shape almost overnight and the large power blocs choosing up sides, the separatist tendencies of small, contrary racial groups, like the Basques, the Catalans, and the Galicians in Spain, have come to seem more and more unrealistic, if not downright comic. The Irish got in under the wire — their cause was just, and they had behind them a history of persecution and stubbornness — but the nationalist parties in Wales and Scotland, for example, have become more or less a refuge for grousers and crackpots. While I was growing up in Scotland, the clishmaclaver of aggressive nationalism rang continuously in my ears, but when I had exhausted the roles of terrorist, martyr, agitator, and cold logician, I found that, after all, it was possible to live quite fruitfully under what we used to call "the English yoke," and that the persecution we suffered was either statistically hypothetical or romantically imagined. I was at first disinclined to take Basque nationalism any more seriously, particularly since, in argument, I often surprised on the faces of my Basque friends the same wistful, faraway expression that I was well used to seeing in Scotland, and also since history shows the Basques to have been defensively, rather than aggressively, nationalistic. By now, however, I have changed my mind. One day I found, tucked into my notebook, a small card. I had no idea how it got there. On one side of it was printed the Basque national hymn and the legend *Euzkadi Es la Patria de los Vascos,* and on the other a very specific Basque Doctrine, some of the main points of which are worthy of note:

The land of the Basques is Euzkadi.

Politically, some Basques are Spanish citizens, the rest French citizens, but originally and by natural law they are neither French nor Spanish. All are, quite simply, Basque.

The French and Spanish languages have their common origin in the breakup of Latin. The true language of the Basque race is

Euzkera, or Basque, utterly distinct in grammar and vocabulary from French and Spanish.

Political and social organization amongst the Basques was determined by their own laws, drawn up by and for themselves, without interference from any foreign power.

Our country has since lost its ancient right to self-government. The results have been disastrous. The purity of the language has been corrupted by Latin influence. The body and soul of the Basque race are in danger of dying out.

The remedy is for all Basques to unite in faith behind their ancient theme of "GOD AND THE OLD LAWS"; that is, to practice their religion faithfully and without corruption, and to reunite in recovering their ancient sovereignty, in a free confederation of the race and of a sovereign Euzkadi.

I showed the card to my friends, and they smiled mysteriously. "That will do as your passport while you are here," they said. "Only, don't show it to the Guardia Civil, or it will get you into trouble." (Basques have a sharp animosity toward the Spanish Civil Guard, whom they regard as foreign troops on their soil. By tacit agreement, no Basque ever joins them, just as few Basques ever serve as career soldiers in the Spanish Army, for that would be to give official Spain a recognition that Basques withhold as far as they can.) Traditionally, all Basques subscribe to the spirit of the Basque Doctrine; to them it is part and parcel of being Basque. The Old Laws constantly invoked in all Basque documents were local *fueros,* or charters, granted in the course of the Middle Ages to particular provinces, or even to small districts, allowing them a complete local autonomy of law and custom, in exchange for which they would lend a judicious allegiance to the Kings of France and Castile. The rights granted by these *fueros* were gradually formalized and codified, and the Basques put all their energies into defending them vigorously. With the French Revolution, the *fueros* of the French Basques disappeared; in Spain they lasted much longer — until after the Carlist Wars of the nineteenth century, when the Basques made the grave mistake of backing the losing side and in the wake of which they seemed to have lost all chance of ever recovering their separate privileges. Nationalism, however, is likely to survive most strongly in the face of persecution and apparent hopelessness; besides, the Basques had too long a tradition of self-esteem ever to allow themselves to subside or to blend easily into any other racial or political circumstance. This history is not peculiar to the Basques, but what interested me most was to discover how the spirit of the *fueros* stood up to the tangled present in Spain.

Generalísimo Franco came away from the agonies of the Civil War with Spain in his pocket — a narrow, dark place, where he has been content enough to let it lie, safe from fresh air. His rule has been marked by a nimble political ingenuity and, at the same time, by an extremely sharp sense of the Spanish character; he has played systematically on the insecurities and self-doubts of Spaniards in the wake of the Civil War, and has kept them so much at the mercy of their own impotence that, with typical two-mindedness, they regard his implacable face on stamps and coins and in public places with explosive hatred and secret relief. Over the years, however, he has been unable to conceal a particularly vituperative hatred of the Basques; his local administration — in the province of Vizcaya in particular — has been brutally repressive. Guernica remains as vivid in his memory as it does in that of the inhabitants.

The main reason for this hatred is that if it were not for the Basques, Franco's slate would look a lot cleaner than it does. His moral justification for the campaign that sparked the Civil War was that he was undertaking a religious crusade as Defender of the Faith; an obvious flaw in his argument was the fact that his bitterest opponents were the Basques, the most devoutly and naturally religious of all Spaniards. If he had in fact been defending the Faith, the Basques would have been likely to be the first to join him. In remaining to this day his bitterest opponents, they flaw even his self-justification.

Since the war, Franco has been able to maintain an uneasy but unbroken alliance with the Spanish Church, out of a mutual need, but at the same time the Basque priests, ruthlessly and sincerely Catholic, and closely concerned with the well-being of their own people, have consistently shaken off his patronage. In May, 1960, a letter signed by three hundred and forty-two of them was presented to the bishops of Vitoria, San Sebastián, Bilbao, and Pamplona, in the four Spanish Basque provinces. The letter was a noble document of conscience, clear, sincere, and to the point. It denounced, bitterly and outspokenly, all forms of social injustice under the Franco regime, coming down heavily on the continuing political imprisonment without trial, the repression of truth and information, and the censorship of the written word, and toward the end it added, on a characteristic note, "We also denounce, before Spaniards and before the rest of the world, the current policy in Spain, whereby, either through neglect or by downright persecution, those ethnic, social, and linguistic characteristics that God granted to the Basques are brushed aside." Franco is well versed in dealing with all forms of political opposition, but such a blunt piece of denunciation coming from priests — and especially from Basque priests — must have stung not only the General but the conscience of the Spanish Church, his uncomfortable ally.

I have listened to countless diatribes against Franco in Madrid, waiting for them to end, as they always do, in a despairing shrug of helplessness. The Basques scarcely bother to mention Franco's name; their contempt is cold, silent, final. "What if the little acorn lives to be a hundred and fifty?" they say. "We'll live longer." The present state of Spain, the Basques feel, is in no sense their fault, nor is it their doom. Being Basque allows them to remain aloof from it, especially since being Basque means to them that they are natural aristocrats, more industrious, more durable, more genuinely religious, more single-minded, less peninsular, and less easily cowed than the rest of Spain.

Nationalists are often their own worst enemies — they are wont to quarrel amongst themselves over the crumbs while neglecting to verify whether or not the loaf is still there. The Basques are not immune from such squabblings. Ever since Basque independence was recognized by the Republic in 1936, an official Basque government-in-exile has maintained itself, first in the United States and now in Paris, and immediately across the Spanish frontier, in Saint-Jean-de-Luz and Biarritz, small clusters of exiles gather to plot, to hope, and to argue. Spanish exiles, as a rule, are like characters in an outdated play — unhappy, remote, and unnaturally wishful. For them, Spain as a reality ended with the Civil War, and they are incapable of understanding that the country has somehow emerged and gone on, however haltingly. They maintain a doubtful aristocracy of memory; beneath it, they are uneasily aware of their own historical pointlessness, and inhabit either a lost past or an improbable future. The Basque exiles with whom I spoke are in a happier position; many of them are able to live freely in France, among Basques, on the very edge of Spain. "We are much more in touch with what is going on in Bilbao and San Sebastián now than when we actually lived there," one of them told me. "As a result, we are much more respectful of the realities of the situation."

What these realities are is not so easy to discover — the Basques are argumentatively fractious and violently extreme in their political gestures. I was invited one evening in Bilbao to a meeting of "influential Basques," and climbed with some trepidation to the top floor of a crumbling old apartment building, where I found a group of about a dozen people sitting around a fire. The apartment was sumptuously furnished, and looked out across the yellow, muddied waters of the Nervión River, which flows from the city to the sea. My host, a member of a prominent industrial family, took me to the window to show me the glare in the sky from the enormous ovens of the Altos Hornos steelworks, downriver. At first sight, Bilbao is memorably ugly, cramped, dirty, and unplanned, but after one has spent some time in it the ugliness gives way to the feel of its sheer force, a kind of seething undercurrent of brawny vigor. Although it is less purely Basque than San Sebastián, it stands as the Goliath of the Basque provinces, and gives the economic backing to all their separatist arguments.

My host waved an arm at the murky river. "If we weren't Basques, we'd be Communists," he said, "because all that you see, and don't see, between Bilbao and the sea is a grotesque injustice — steelworks, shipyards, factories owned by a handful of people, their ludicrous mansions occupied a few weeks out of the year, and the workers cramped in dingy tenements, underemployed, desperate. Bilbao ought to make us feel more uncomfortable than we do, for, as Basques, we have always claimed to be equally endowed with nobility and humanity. But we're very much aware of the power we have, and of the fear that Franco has of us. When the time comes, we'll be ready."

The conversation I listened to was charged with high excitement and had nothing of the despairing languor I was used to in Madrid. Politically, the points of view varied to the extremes of anarchy, but they had in common an assured confidence — the Basque conviction of the inevitability of events, the long, patient perspective. At one point, an old, white-haired man sat down beside me to explain the company, his sharp chin thrusting forward as he spoke. (The prominent Basque nose is famous, but it is the hooked chin, leading forward and jerking up in emphasis, that I find distinguishes the Basques as they talk. On the medallions sold in the souvenir shops, the tilting beret, the long nose, and the curling chin of the profiles seem to be converging to a single point.)

"Perhaps, if you're not used to us, you shouldn't listen too closely," said the old man. "Me, I've been a Basque nationalist all my life — only now we talk not of nationalism or separatism but of auto-determination. But it's all the same — and I'm accustomed to these escapes of steam, for we Basques have plenty of it. Among the Basques in San Sebastián you'll have found the romantics, the dreamers; here in Bilbao we are the hardheaded ones. Oh, we have Communists and Socialists and Republicans, and even a few monarchists; our politics are as mixed as you'll find anywhere in Spain. The difference is that we are Basques, and you can be sure of this — that if anything begins to happen in Spain, if there appears the least crack in the surface, we'll all become Basques at once, and we'll *take* our independence this time, firmly, with both hands. We have power, we have money, we work hard, and we have no lack of confidence. If Spain had treated us as France has treated the French Basques, we might have stayed Spaniards. But we've had our share of persecution — Franco has done everything possible to keep us from speaking our own language, for instance — and the consequences are inevitable, and not very far away. If it were not for Franco, the Basque country might be nothing more than a museum by now. Well, we're far from being moth-eaten. You'll see."

When we returned to the conversation, it had lost its serious edge and become more normally ludicrous. A Madrid-born architect who had settled in Bilbao was declaring himself a firm anti-Basque and was threatening to found a society for the suppression of Basques, to the delight of the others. "Living here, I've grown sick of everything Basque," he was telling them. "If I had my way, I'd ban the beret, change all the names, make it a punishable offense to speak that impossible language, forbid folk dancing and pelota, and try to get you all back to a semblance of ordinary human life. You're all blood-mad. You wouldn't marry Brigitte Bardot unless you found at least five Basques in her family tree. I wish you would get your independence, because then we could fence off the Basque country as a kind of zoo for tourists. As it is, I'll never move forward one step in Bilbao unless I change my name to Machimbarrena or Zulizarreta."

The others applauded him enthusiastically.

"The thing is, he's quite right," the old man said. "If you aren't a Basque and happen to live among us, we'll drive you mad. We have a racial superiority complex, if you like. Perhaps we are no more than relics and freaks to the outside eye, but we haven't just preserved the trappings and manners of a race; we've kept alive a whole way of being. We don't really need to write out the Basque Doctrine and the Old Laws. We know them all in our bones. The stupidest thing that Spain does is to tell us repeatedly that Euzkadi doesn't exist."

Now an easy humor predominated; the rest of the conversation was quick and witty, and brimmed over with the restless, glancing energy that can keep a Basque talking all night without noticing it.

In a sharp essay on the Basque character, Ortega y Gasset went after this very self-confidence. "The Basque thinks that the mere fact of having been born and of being a human individual gives him all the value that it is possible for one to have in this world," he wrote. "All the superior qualities and perfections rising above the level of the elementally human are for the Basque poor, negligible excrescences. The great, the valuable in man is what is most lowly and aboriginal, the subterranean, that which keeps him tied to the earth. Since history is above all a competition and a dispute and rivalry to acquire those superfluous and superficial perfections — knowledge, art, political dominion — it is not surprising that the Basque race has taken so little interest in history."

With all due respect to Ortega, he measured the Basques against the wrong scale — and not surprisingly, because they can be measured against no scale but the one they themselves set. In truth, they are not so much nationalists or separatists as localists; they have no large, cohesive political ambitions to equal the one desire they are born with—to remain utterly local, individual, and particular. I doubt very much whether the Basque Republic, should it come to pass again, would ever bother about being represented on the international scene. As long as each village was allowed its distinctness, each individual his mannerisms, Basques would feel little need for constituent assemblies. This utter particularity is what makes them unaccountable, and can make them exasperating. They are quite happy to defy analysis, since analysis, they feel, might begin to infringe on their oddness.

The proof of all this is in that famous language, unapproachable though it is even to anyone with a good ear and a healthy grounding in the civilized languages of the world. It is pleasant to listen to as sheer sound, but there is not even a very occasional tinkle of resemblance to allow one to catch a thread of the sense; for anyone not born and bred a Basque, it remains pretty finally out of reach. Basque is almost entirely devoid of abstract terms; it is structurally agglutinative, forming concepts by an accretion of particular elements. Its few abstract nouns are all late borrowings from Latin; while it has a separate noun for every kind of tree found in the Basque provinces, the word for "tree" itself is comparatively recent. Its prevalent *k*'s and *x*'s and *z*'s give it a bizarre look on the page; the street signs in the fishing village of Deva, enamelled in both Basque and Spanish, gave me an awesome sense of the gulf between the two languages. I have waited patiently in small village inns while old men pawed through their tattered Basque-Spanish dictionaries to find a word that might put us even faintly in touch with one another, and in all my time in the Basque country I think I have learned to say no more than nine Basque words — hardly an encouraging beginning. After a time, however, it is the surnames that first become familiar — Barandiarán, Etcheverría, Arantzazu — and the strange place names. I came one morning upon a village with the odd name of Ea, and when I stopped there for some food, it was to discover that in Basque, as happens often enough, the village had a different name entirely. Its Basque name was Ie. It is the language, finally, that leaves non-Basques forever on the outside of the mystery. A few incursions are possible, for Basque is thickly onomatopoeic (*"bimbi-bimbaka"* refers to the pealing of bells, *"gili-gili"* means "tickling," *"irrintzi"* is the noun for the neighing of horses), but beyond the physical pleasure of these words the stranger must stay mumchance and dumfounded.

Even so, it is not the oddness of the language, or even the careful avoidance of the abstract, that accounts for the aura of mystery that Basques seem to wear about them. Once I had stopped attempting to recognize Euzkadi either as part of France or as part of Spain, it began to seem to me like a curious nowhere, to which neither time nor judgment could ever apply. Often, at evening, when the sun laid a reddish-gold light on the small deep-green fists of hills, on the tidy fields and farmyards, all beautifully touched by human hand, and when the quick, soft talk started up in the inns, I found myself wondering where on the map I could possibly be — if, indeed, I was traceable on any map at all. I began to notice, a long way off, the clop of horses, the cries of goosegirls gathering up the geese with their long, handcarved crooks, the screech of winches in the fishing villages; and the sounds, recurring and recurring, gradually began to pry me loose from all contexts other than this small nutshell of leftover life. My friends there often amused themselves by telling me wild, improbable tales of the *lamiñak*, the race of ghostly night visitors whom Basques charge with the responsibility for all strange happenings. Bit by bit, I found myself easily believing every word. Even in as urbane a setting as San Sebastián, the summer capital of Spain, fringed with the international set and the shades of touring royalty (Queen Victoria visited San Sebastián in 1889, and complained to her diary that she found the tea served her by the Queen Regent of Spain "quite undrinkable") — even there, in the ham-hung, shell-strewn bars by the harbor, a song is likely to arise suddenly and spontaneously from a small knot of fishermen, a song so rare, so eerily remote, that it entirely obliterates the bar, the evening, and the listening ears. More than once, listening to the wailing of the weird, flutelike *tchirula*, I have shivered involuntarily. The longer I have stayed, the less like Spain it has all become; instead of the cheerful, shrugging carelessness of the Spaniards, I keep surprising a remote, ancestral look on the carved Basque faces. The next instant, however, it has disappeared, and the silence has given way to a torrent of comic preposterousness.

By now, my double, Lorenzo, has probably gone back to sea. I remember the remark of the old man in Guernica about the Pyrenees. From my window I am just able to see them, scribbled jaggedly along the skyline. At this moment, they may even be alive with Basques, moving nimbly and unhampered between the two halves of Euzkadi. From here, on this hazy evening, the mountains look not only implacably durable but very, very old.

Barcelona — 1961

"DON'T ask me how I am," grumbled the driver as I climbed into the yellow taxi. "And don't tell me it's hot. And please don't say you want to be taken to the football stadium or the bull ring in a hurry."

I reassured him, and he sighed as only taxi-drivers can sigh — a long escaping hiss of world-weary air, like a deflating tire.

"Just in case you think I'm badly educated, I'll tell you what I've done today, and you can judge for yourself whether I'm mad or not," he went on. "It being both Sunday and a fiesta, I took my family very early to the seashore. It was beautiful there, and I soaked my feet in the sea. But since then I've taken priests to the exhibition of Romanesque art at the Palacio Nacional and brought back boys from the bicycle races. I drove five French singers to the Festival of Popular Song, and I took two Moors in fancy dress to the morning procession. I drove a Belgian cyclist to his hotel — what does a cyclist want with a taxi when he has an estimable bicycle of his own? I had a bite in the taxi between the Exhibition of Old Cars and the Stamp Market, and then I started ferrying people out to the football stadium, picking up others bound for the bullfight on the way back. I've been three times to the stadium and twice to the bull ring, with everybody telling me to hurry; what's more, half the streets are closed off and the traffic police are all in a bad mood. And before long I'll have to be back at the stadium to catch the football crowd, and then the leftovers from the bull-fight, and I still have to get to the seashore in time to fetch my family for the procession this evening, or my children will never forgive me. And I'd like to put my feet in the sea just once more," he added wistfully.

Reflecting that nationality makes little or no difference in the temperament of taxi-drivers, I assured him that I was only go-ing to see a friend; it was, however, anything but a reassurance.

"There's an athletic match going on between Spain and Aus-tria that I haven't been to yet," he told me. "Are you sure you don't want to see it? I can easily get some visitor to bring back from the lunatic asylum close by, and I still have time for a couple of museums or the Book Fair before the football's over. I wouldn't mind being at any one of these things myself, but I probably should be in the lunatic asylum. You're sure you want to visit this friend? It seems so tame, for the Merced."

It *was* tame for the Merced — the Feast of Nuestra Señora de la Merced, the patroness of Barcelona, who first descended in the year of 1218 to assume the inspirational responsibility for the people of the city, and in whose honor Barcelona plunges into a week of extravagant pageantry every autumn. So many events were announced each day in *La Vanguardia,* the morning paper, that just reading them over I felt tired; not so the citizenry, who stepped up their normally hectic pace and turned out everywhere in such numbers that nobody could have been left at home but a smattering of invalids and crones.

That evening, I waited about for an hour on the broad, graceful, and well-heeled Paseo de Gracia for the evening procession to come, in a jostling, bright-eyed crowd that seemed not to care very much whether it arrived or not. Children fell asleep on their parents' shoulders; the police conferred with one another; everyone smiled at everyone else; and banter flew extravagantly about. When the procession did arrive, heralded by successive waves of gasping, murmuring, and cheering, it proved to be a series of floats of a comic commercio-religious blend, half soft sell, half sanctity; I found myself gazing at what I took to be Our Lady of the Coca-Colas, hurling streamers into the crowd. "It's not Ave Maria, it's Avecrem," said a man in front of me. (Avecrem is a dehydrated Spanish soup that has initiated Spaniards into the *mythos* of latter-day advertising.) Commerce carried the night, and I watched the *Santa María*, the *Niña*, and the *Pinta* cruise past in turn, built, it seemed to me, of sugar. The children were awake and shouting. A platoon of motorcycle police followed on the hoofs of a mounted guard, and a vintage fire engine clattered after them, smoking, and clanging its brass bell. Paper streamers hung from the floodlit, super-green plane trees. People filtered in and out of the ragged edge of the crowd, peering on tiptoe, chattering, and, by now, yawning. I withdrew to a café, which slowly filled up around me, even though it was striking midnight. The mood of the day showed no sign of fizzing out, and somewhere not far off I could hear the *piff-paff* of fireworks. Following the crowds, I took a walk down the

Ramblas, the series of leafy boulevards that leads from the center of Barcelona all the way to the harbor. Shoeshiners were still on their knees, polishing away, and old men sat on the benches serenely, as if it were noon and not midnight. In Barcelona, the Ramblas belong to everyone; books are written about them, poems pay homage to them, songs celebrate them, and all Barcelonans help to walk them smooth at least one night of the seven, winter or summer, when they have time, which they always have. The shoeshiners patrol them like a private army; a cluster of stalls sells flowers by the armful, birds in boxes, and even monkeys. The Ramblas scarcely ever sleep, for soon after dawn the daily boat from Majorca puts in and the bleary travellers force open the cafés, which this evening were in the excited custody of men replaying the football match in loud voices or sitting in gloomy judgment on the afternoon's bullfight. I turned into one of the small street corridors that wind away from the Ramblas; along it a few unlikely shops were still open, not so much for purposes of trade as out of sheer amiability, and the small familial bars were crowded and agog. Nobody seemed tired, or even looked it.

Often, toward evening, I lost myself in that same labyrinth of small streets half deliberately, so as to whet my curiosity. The cramped shops follow one another in tight succession, their fronts great arches, open or glassed, letting in light and air from the street, each shop a dimly lit stage-set, each presenting an improbable scene from an unlikely play, soundlessly and eerily. An old woman knits in the corner of an antique shop, under tottering heaps of old brass, with the shadows thrown by chipped statues splayed grotesquely across the vaulted ceiling; an old, bent philatelist peers from his lair, mumbling of perforations and watermarks. Small restaurants and *tascas* wear their menus chalked on their doors — squid, mussels, indiscrim-

inate fish dishes. From dark doorways, the outposts of Barcelona's multifarious small industries, saws whine and acetylene
torches sputter. The smells swamp one another — mothballs,
clean laundry, stale marzipan, and the reasty odor of wine-
soaked wood from dark bodegas. Every now and then, a quiet
square crops up, with someone asleep in a corner.

The air has the faintest suggestion of autumn in it. A few
leaves fall from the plane trees and scuttle in the dust; the
damp seeps into the city from the sea. Between Tibidabo, the
low mountain toward which the city climbs (and the legendary
scene of Christ's Temptation by Satan), and the broad reaches
of the harbor, Barcelona spreads out in a checkerboard of
streets, crossed and complicated by four or five broad avenues.
Fountains grace the more important intersections, but a block
away from them long gonfalons of laundry may be draped
from the upper windows. Often, the boom of a ship's siren
rises above the clatter of streetcars; small ferries, never empty,
crisscross the harbor, back and forth to the lighthouse at its
extremity. For the week of the Merced, a number of small fairs
have sprung up on dusty vacant lots all over the city, their
roundabouts never wanting for children, their ancient photog-
raphers never lacking victims; and at evening, in the various
barrios of the city, the locals flock to a preappointed square to
dance the *sardana*, the national dance of Catalonia, so intricate that the dancers still count breathlessly as they thread
through the mazes of one another's movements. The Merced
means bullfights every day, exhibitions, processions, contests,
festivals, *sardanas* in the evening, window displays, and what-
not. "But," said the hotel doorman one morning, "the truth is
that we do this all year long, only this week we announce it
in the newspapers."

I doubt whether anyone would call Barcelona a beautiful

city; the issue never comes up, for there is not time to consider it. The city is too rambunctious to pause for so effete an assessment; it *goes,* with all the most recent implications of the verb. Old as it is, it never rests on its history; modern as it sees itself, it has not arrived or levelled off but still presses ruthlessly on, stranding some of its elements anachronistically behind yet keeping to a bold, energetic physical pulse. Curiosities abound in its backwaters, but in the foreground it is busy pushing on to bigger and, one must suppose, better things, at a thoroughly un-Spanish pace.

As the capital of Catalonia, the rich northeastern corner of Spain that comprises the four provinces of Lérida, Gerona, Barcelona, and Tarragona, Barcelona has had two histories: a long and honorable one that began in 230 B.C., when it became an important Carthaginian settlement, and that extended through its centuries of influence as a rich trading port of the western Mediterranean; and a short, violent one that started with the sudden industrialization of the city and its surroundings in the second half of last century, ran through a series of political eruptions, culminated in the political autonomy of Catalonia, granted in 1932, and ended abruptly with the fall of Barcelona at the termination of the Spanish Civil War. The Carthaginian city is said to have been settled by Hamilcar Barca, about 230 B.C., and was called Barcino after him; the port was prized by the Romans, who came along thirty years later, as their most important western outpost. It was conquered by the Moors in 713, and later annexed to the Kingdom of Aragon; in 1640 it rejected the rule of Philip IV and allied itself with the France of Richelieu and Mazarin for an unhappy twelve years. But throughout all these comings and goings — the wars between Castile and Aragon and, later, between Spain and

[98]

France — the Catalans went their steady, self-sufficient way, rich in natural resources, industrious and adaptable in temperament, independent in character. The wealth and energy of Catalonia were always thoroughly appreciated by the Spanish kings; at the same time, however, its independence of spirit was a steady source of disquiet to them. In the Middle Ages, as a maritime city-state, Barcelona enjoyed a prosperity much like that of Genoa, Marseille, and Venice (its code of trade, the *Libro del Consulado del Mar*, was held in great respect throughout the Mediterranean as a definition of fair practice), and it continued to do so until the sixteenth century, when, oddly enough, it lost much of its mercantile importance with the discovery of America, which placed it suddenly at an uncomfortable distance from the New World. This history is well preserved in the city's neat museums; the changing maps show its steady march back from the harbor toward Tibidabo. Its latter-day expansion to the north and south has been the result of industrialization, and now its citizens grumble that if its adjacent suburbs were properly taken into account its population would number substantially more than two million, and that since it would then be bigger than Madrid, the capital, this cannot be allowed to happen officially.

The second, drastic history of Barcelona began with its emergence as one of the two great industrial cities of Spain (Bilbao is the other) and as the country's principal modern seaport. The growing textile industry created a new working class and, with it, a rich bourgeoisie, in contrast to the rest of Spain, which even today is markedly feudal, with peasants who work the land in much the same way they always have and a rash of rich, indolent landlords. Toward the end of the last century, Barcelona bloomed and blossomed and began to give birth to great ambitions. Catalonia had its own language and

[99]

culture; it was prospering fast, independent of Madrid, for which it felt a deep contempt and resentment; it was in touch with the rest of Europe; and it saw itself as the most advanced and responsible region of Spain, hampered only by the strings that tied it to Castile. It was inevitable that this new zeal should sooner or later bring it into conflict with the central government, and it was just as inevitable that the workers, as they discussed and devoured all forms of new ideas and felt some glimmerings of the possibilities ahead, should come into violent conflict with the new middle class — the factory owners and managers — in a prolonged struggle for rights and privileges. But what was less predictable was the form that this revolutionary zeal took. In the eighteen-sixties, an Italian called Fanelli arrived in Spain and began to preach the Anarchist ideals of Bakunin. They spread like a fever and took a firm hold on the working class in Barcelona, which became the home of the Spanish Anarchist movement — a movement that at the beginning of the Civil War numbered close to a million and a half adherents and that had infinitely more appeal and importance in Spain than Socialism or Communism. This is perhaps not too difficult to understand; Bakunin's ruling notion of the state as an evil is something that is almost an instinct amongst Spaniards, and his insistence on the need for violent action against authority gave the workers an ideological justification for the inflammable rancor that was running in their veins. By the turn of the century, the Barcelona Anarchists were beginning to lay about them in a series of riots, assassinations, and demonstrations that continued into and throughout the Civil War; they directed their flagrant hatred against the middle class and the clergy, and although they were emphatically on the side of the Republic when war came, they conducted their own campaign against their private enemies

to such effect that the Civil War reflected an even more confused complexity in Barcelona than it did elsewhere on the
Peninsula.

From the turn of the century on, the new forces that had
been building up in Catalonia began to join together in a
general movement toward separation from the rest of Spain,
for by that time Catalan nationalism had the three solid foundations necessary to support it as a serious movement: a separate language, literature, and culture, all in a healthy condition;
an economic potential that could easily sustain Catalonia on
its own; and a political current that was running in a new,
independent direction. Moreover, separatism gave the dispa-
rate groups in Catalonia a central point around which they
could unite and act, instead of fighting among themselves.
Strikes and open rebellion were never far from the surface —
1909 saw a week of savage rioting and church-burning in
Barcelona, and in 1917 a fierce strike spread from Catalonia
across the rest of the country — and order had always to be
kept by strict policing by the Army, which only augmented
separatist feelings. When, in 1931, the Spanish Republic was
finally proclaimed, "the Catalan question" was one of the first,
most pressing problems on its plate, and it was wise enough
to settle the question as promptly as it could, passing in the
summer of 1932 the Catalan Statute, which granted limited
powers of self-government to Catalonia, though keeping it
within the broad jurisdiction of the Republic. At first flush,
the statute was to the Catalans a triumph of a kind, but it
satisfied nobody — neither the absolutists, who wished to keep
Spain firmly united, nor the workers, who saw it as a watery
compromise on the part of the rich industrialists. In 1934, Luis
Companys, the Catalan nationalist leader, fearing that the
Republic was falling under the control of monarchists and

Fascists, set in motion a further Catalan rebellion, with the end of securing more autonomy and more separation, but the rebellion was quickly crushed by the Army — tragically enough, for if it had succeeded it might have made a great difference to subsequent Spanish history. When the Civil War did break out, in July, 1936, with the Army rising led by General Franco, it was marked in Barcelona by a day of bitter fighting. The workers armed themselves, the Civil Guard, uncharacteristically, joined them, and the Army forces were bloodily subdued; this left Barcelona as one of the principal strongholds of the Republic, but left it still riddled by internal hatreds and frictions that make the brief history of the Catalan state read like a tragedy within a tragedy.

In Barcelona, I spoke to many people who remembered that day, July 19, 1936, when the bullets pinged off the walls on the Ramblas, and the dead men and horses piled up in the Plaza de Cataluña, the center of the fighting (as now — well-groomed and fountained, rimmed with new neon — it is the placid center for the evening *paseo*), and who remembered also the entry into the silent, deserted streets of the city, on January 26, 1939, of the Nationalist troops, a few hours after the remnants of the Republican Army and the rags and tatters of the government had fled to the north and exile. It is unlikely that, even with time, Spain will ever have its Civil War "buffs." In the United States, it is only the character and remoteness of its Civil War that make such minute interest possible; in Spain, even at a remove of twenty-odd years, the memory is too cruel, too savage, too crippling, too shameful, and too dangerous to be revived. Nor is the Spanish Civil War ever likely to give rise to a wave of literature or analysis, for the new generation of writers in Spain consists of those who are young enough not to be emasculated by the memory of the war. When Spaniards speak of it, they do so with a curious hush in their voices, as though they doubted whether it actually happened, hoping, perhaps, that it never did. (Spaniards are exceptionally prone to the belief that if something is not mentioned it may just cease to exist.) The Civil War, however, branded itself so bitterly on the memories of those who lived through it that in order to go on at all with the business of human life they have had to sever all connection in their minds between the present and the past — a state of affairs that has left the older generation foundered in tragic discontinuity, plagued by bad dreams and a melancholy sense of its own helplessness.

I expected, even now, to find some of the old political impulses still alive, particularly since Franco's regime looks on Barcelona as a trouble center, because of its concentration of industrial workers and its record of illegal strikes in the wake of the Second World War. Instead, I found quite the reverse. I ran into a few Catalan nationalists, but they were of the wistful, romantic persuasion, and themselves looked on their aspirations as minor, cultural ones. Anarchism, I was assured, still had a horde of phantom listeners, even more distant now from the hard realities of the Spanish situation than they used to be. Socialists and Communists were active, but most of the people I spoke to shrugged them into insignificance. Franco's regime has remained in power so long and with such implacable solidity that most Catalans have given up politics as a pointless luxury and have focussed their attention on their immediate economic situation.

"Even five years ago, we were on fire," a mechanic told me. "Strikes were always in the wind, and we were ready for anything. But it has changed. What's the use of striking now, when it'll only mean we lose our jobs, if we don't go to prison?

In Barcelona, we're lucky, because there's enough work, and we concentrate on picking up a little extra, always a bit more. The truth is we're too busy to strike. And what's the use of playing politics, when we're not allowed parties or open discussion? That's for fools. And don't think we're sorry for ourselves, either. We think we're lucky. Every year it gets a bit better, and, for my part, I'd rather work than grumble. I won't say that if a local Fidel Castro came along I wouldn't grow a beard and join him. But I can tell you that now I'd think twice about doing it, whereas a few years ago I was ready to burn down my grandmother."

The more familiar I become with the elusive facts of Spanish economics, the clearer it grows that the survival of the country and its inhabitants fully justifies their belief in *el milagro español,* for it cannot be understood as anything less than a miracle. Even with two jobs and a good fifteen-hour workday, Spanish *obreros* cannot explain to themselves how they keep fed and clothed, let alone divert themselves as regularly as they do at the movies, the football matches, and the bullfights, all of which they use to keep their minds off their disastrously evanescent future. But survive they do. Not that they never complain — scratch a Spaniard on the subject of money and you start up a flood of rhetorical questions and eloquent gestures. But nevertheless, on they go, teetering barefoot into Europe's new steel-and-glass age, apparently without a worry in their heads, and with scarcely more than a peseta in their pockets. Except that "teetering" would hardly be the word for the Catalans, who are less bothered by metaphysical preoccupations and more inclined to get on with the business at hand. Other Spaniards tell you that Catalans have to be watched closely — they have a reputation for commercial hardheadedness not unlike that of the Lowland Scots, and they probably deserve it — but the accusation is made mostly because they give up a good part of their time to making money (an activity that would never occur to an Andalusian), and the pursuit of money has never brought out the more human and sympathetic side of any character, national or individual. It is not only in business that Catalans are impatient and active; they charge into the arts with the same industrious curiosity, unabashedly physical, naïvely enthusiastic, making the languid sophistication of Madrid look effete by comparison. And it is. Barcelona, unlike other Spanish cities, looks and acts like a real city instead of an overgrown provincial capital; it is proud of itself, and does not care who knows it. If Castile embodies the transcendental future of Spain and the North the solid, proud past, Catalonia is its energetic present, eagerly adaptable, ready for anything.

For the past twelve years, the economy of Spain has been kept afloat, or at least sluggishly awash, by having vast amounts of money pumped into it regularly, mostly by the United States. Since foreign aid has made no noticeable difference in the context of individual life (Spaniards credit the United States with little more than subsidizing the erection of public monuments to Franco's regime), the people personally have kept themselves afloat by whatever means they can. (Spain and Spaniards have to be mentioned separately, because Spaniards themselves insist on the distinction; since they are given no responsibility under the regime that governs them, they take none, making the point that their personal *bien estar* is something they achieve in spite of Franco.) When they forget themselves long enough to look ahead — apart from saying that things cannot possibly go on as they are, which has been said in Spain for centuries — they realize that the kind of isolated superiority they have claimed for themselves in the past is now precarious and unrealistic, and the most hopeful prospect is that, in time, Spain will worm its way into the new European community, probably as an apprentice member, since it has little to offer the booming countries to the north except non-exportable sunshine. Characteristically, the Catalans, although they would not admit ever to having considered the matter, appear some time ago to have accepted this state of affairs; in the ten years that I have known Barcelona, it has grown more noticeably European in appearance. The journey down from France is not the violent transition it once was; the place has learned from its tourists, and its eye turns amiably toward the north. Even its traditional scorn for Madrid has lost its edge, except on the football field. To cut the Catalans down to size, Castile used to say that Spain began at the Ebro (the river that forms the southern border of Catalonia) and that the Catalans were not Spaniards at all. The saying now has a new significance. "Here we already have our feet in Europe," remarked one Catalan businessman. "Soon enough Madrid will be running to us, instead of making us run to it. The prospect of being Europeans first and Spaniards second doesn't worry us nearly as much as it worries the rest. If it means we can live better — well, good; let's get on with it."

These days, Barcelona can hardly claim, as it once could and still tries to, that it supports the rest of Spain, for it does not now enjoy the splendid industrial isolation it did even thirty years ago. What it can take credit for, however, is attracting a large slice of the tourist industry, which, even allowing for the fanciful nature of official statistics, is far and away the most important source of foreign income for the whole Peninsula. For tourists, Barcelona is a kind of sieve.

They pour into it by road from France, from the high seas, and from the air, spending a few days as they arrive or leave; they have even taken to holding conventions in the city. North of Barcelona lies the Costa Brava, haunt of occasional writers and painters, beat of the international set, and paradise for tireless English tourists in blazers and summer chintz, dazed with joy to discover that the sun that shines on celebrities may also shine reliably on them. It would be silly to suppose that tourism has left Spain untouched, particularly now that it has reached such staggering proportions. (The *Dirección General del Turismo* announced that eight million tourists had already crossed the frontier in 1961, and that two million more would do so before the year burned out.) Tourism certainly provides an invisible foreign income that allows the Economic Ministry to make its balance of payments look a lot healthier than it is. On a more innocent level, though, it makes Spaniards sharply aware of the soaring standard of living in the rest of Europe and gives them a hunger for the *dolce vita* of the Common Market countries. Now, instead of behaving as though the very fact of being in Spain should be enough for anyone to rejoice in, they have seen to it that hot water flows, however falteringly, in the humblest hotels, and gone for good are the mock-English translations on the menus ("plonged egs," "bruised bef," "mixed-up fishes," "Inglish tease"). Although Barcelona has a year-round quota of French, German, and English tourists, they are not conspicuous; the local population saunters just as they do, slowly and agape, and on Sundays the cars streaming to the French frontier, two hundred kilometres to the north, mostly carry Barcelona licenses.

One thing about Barcelona that sets it apart from other towns in Spain is its profusion of bookshops. Elsewhere, one mostly comes across dim newspaper shops selling dried-out erasers, religious comic books, and embroidered postcards, with a scanty shelf of books somewhere in the back, most of which turn out to be racy Spanish translations of Zane Grey and Somerset Maugham, the two writers who, by a freak of circumstance, bear on their wordy shoulders the reputation of English literature for non-English-reading Spaniards. In Barcelona, however, one cannot help noticing the proliferating *librerías*, busy and well stocked, with substantial English, French, and German sections. In the kiosks, too, the morning papers, notably *La Vanguardia*, and the magazines like *Destino*, the well-informed Barcelona weekly, sell out promptly. All this would seem to indicate a healthy general appetite for the written word, but the blunt truth is that by the time the written word in Spain reaches the reader it does so in a state of limp emasculation. Just as it is hard to grasp, on the bright, cheerful surface of Spain, the sinister presence of police supervision, so it is at first hard to believe that films, plays, and all forms of writing are scrutinously censored. Slowly, however, the news in the daily papers grows conspicuous by its absence, or if it is there at all, it is muffled in ambiguous prose, shelved on inconspicuous pages, bottled up in dusty, gray articles, stoppered with the mildest of headlines. Occasionally, one hears of telephones being tapped and mail being opened, and although this is not the rule, it happens sufficiently often to be a nuisance and — what is more important to the regime — a deterrent. By showing that it occasionally can, the regime leaves the uneasy impression that it always might, and that is enough for the majority, who are bent on avoiding trouble.

The censorship does not prevent intelligent Spaniards from being as well informed as anybody else, but it does insure that anything printed in Spanish and available to the bulk of the population has had its political and moral ambiguities blue-pencilled well in advance, and this makes book publishing in Spain mountainously difficult. In Barcelona, I spent some time with Carlos Barral, a poet whom I had known in the past and a partner in the Barcelona publishing house of Seix & Barral — by all accounts the most eminent and progressive in Spain. In the last five years, Seix & Barral has put out Spanish translations of a clutch of writers as varied as Lionel Trilling, Alain Robbe-Grillet, Henry Green, Carson McCullers, and Henry Miller, and in 1960 it helped launch the Prix Formentor for novels — an international prize that assures the simultaneous publication of the winning novel in thirteen countries. Barral is young, quick, bearded, and intense; his enterprise has been a focus for the whole younger generation of Spanish poets, critics, and novelists — a generation that by now is beginning to pull itself together and write. Being both adventurous and active as a publisher, Barral has gained plenty of first-hand experience of book censoring. In his office, I spent some time going over mangled manuscripts that had come back from the Central Office for the Inspection of Books, in Madrid — the branch of the Spanish Ministry of Information to which copies of all books, Spanish or foreign, must be sent before publication.

"When we contemplate putting out a French, German, or English book," Barral told me, "we submit it in the original language, since it would certainly not be worth our while to go ahead with a translation unless we had the censor's approval. These books — and any Spanish books we submit — are delegated by the censorship office to readers, who report on them, and after a month or six weeks we are notified of the censor's verdict. Publication is either approved or forbidden or, quite commonly, approved with certain cuts, in which case we have to get in touch with the author to see whether he, in turn, will approve the cuts. If a book is turned down on the first reading, we are allowed to submit it again, accompanied by a statement defending our reasons for wishing to publish it, and justifying whatever moral and political offensiveness it is charged with. This means an even longer wait. As you can see, the whole process takes an exasperating amount of time; for us, publication of a book is the end of a long, long process. But make no mistake — if our firm planned to put out a new edition of *Don Quixote,* we would still have to submit two copies of the text to the censor, although in that instance the chances are that it would go through."

Censorship might have been accepted into Spanish life as an inevitable consequence of the regime, as many injustices and discomforts have been, if it were not for the wild caprice of its application. In November, 1960, a group of over two hundred Spanish writers, artists, intellectuals, and editors sent the Ministries of Information and Education an open letter, heavy with irony, declaring that while the signers realized there was little point in appealing directly for the repeal of censorship, at least some serviceable clarification of its foundations was necessary; it was not enough to claim vaguely that it was preserving the political ideals of the regime and the moral ideals of the Church. I remember hearing one of the signers, a Madrid novelist, complain at the time, "In one book of mine they struck out the word 'red' whenever it appeared. So in my next book I never once used the word — quite an accomplishment, don't you think? But what did they do? They eliminated the word 'thigh' instead. So now I'm contemplating an illicit novel called, provisionally, 'Red Thighs.' It may even get through." In principle, he was quite accurate. In some of the manuscripts I read, strongly worded political passages were left intact, while passages that bore only the faintest traces of human intimacy were heavily excised; in others, it was quite the reverse. (It is not uncommon for the censor to eliminate from a text all mention of the Soviet Union, presumably on the assumption, again, that if a thing is never mentioned in print it may just go away.) Particular censorship appears to be either heavily ecclesiastical or heavily political, with little in between, but in fact the whole basis of censorship is so capricious that the more progressive publishers often try their lot with an uncertain book in the hope of a lucky accident of omission. The most ludicrous example I came across was a novel by the Italian writer Italo Svevo in which the word "bed" had been consistently struck from the text. Since the novel treats of a chronic invalid, the Spanish text reads a trifle starkly. More eerie still, the official response from the censorship office to the publisher mentions neither the title of the book nor the author's name but, instead, refers obliquely to an accompanying sheet of paper, which carries the censor's verdict but no official letterhead or stamp, so that no legal proof of book censorship exists. This is typical official hypocrisy, like the inscrutable smile on the ubiquitous public face of Franco; the actions and methods of the regime are merciless and to the point, but the public apologia is always presented in pompously disarming terms, invoking liberty, morality, God, and the glorious name of Spain. Officially, there is no political imprisonment; actually, prisoners are condemned to nothing more or less than oblivion.

Characteristically, the censor comes down less heavily on limited editions of books published at a price prohibitive enough to insure a small sale. If a Spanish publisher proposed to issue the "Complete Writings of Karl Marx" printed on human skin and bound in morocco, the Madrid office might conceivably let the edition pass. But when, as in the United

States, the only problem is whether or not the written word has taken on itself more freedom than it can responsibly support, the Spanish situation seems a little remote, a little unbelievable in the light of Spain's shining literary tradition. The first problem for a young Spanish writer is not whether anybody will read his book but whether it will get past the clumsy, insentient blue pencil of the censor and still smack of life. A good many of the writers with whom I spoke have reacted by releasing their volubility in endless conversation. Since writing can hold for them little hope either of economic stability or of constructive influence or criticism, they transfer their literary pretensions into a flow of exuberant talk, but with the control of the written word remaining in the hands of a small group of ecclesiastics and state employees, their exuberance is fairly theatrical. I have listened in Spain to more manifestoes in the making than I care to count in my memory, but all of them — letters of protest, appeals, pronouncements — have met with nothing more than the implacable *silencio administrativo,* which leaves no room for recourse, appeal, or action.

One day while I was buying the morning paper on the Ramblas, the news agent was unwrapping a bundle of copies of *Lady Chatterley's Lover,* in English.

"Will you sell them easily?" I asked him.

"Oh, yes, tourists buy them," he replied, "but I wish we had something of our own to sell instead of this, which cannot be very illicit if it is English. I would like to publish my family budget for the last two years. That would make them jump out of their skins, but, poor souls, they come here to have a good time."

As if it were not enough to have to weather the imbecilities of the censorship in order to launch a book on a tiny reading public unused to anything but the placid ambiguities of official prose, the Catalan writer is in an even more gloomy position; Catalan is his true language, and officially he is not even allowed to write in it. "To be a Catalan writer nowadays is like being a sun worshipper in Siberia," one playwright told me. "I've written over thirty plays in Catalan, and even if the censor agreed to consider them, the subject matter would make him hit the roof. Yet what can I do — learn a new language, become a new person? Sometimes I read my plays to a few friends. Their attention is about the only reward I get out of writing, but nevertheless I began a new unpublishable book last week, which will keep me fruitlessly busy for a few months. The last time I submitted a book to the censor, he waited a year and then told me it had disappeared. Being a Catalan writer amounts to talking to yourself. It may be diverting, but it's lonely."

At first sound, the Catalan language seems to be a blunted dialect of Castilian Spanish, but it is actually a quite distinct, fully formed Neo-Latin language, with a long, rich literary past. The Bible was printed in Catalan in 1478; the whole canon of classical literature has been meticulously edited and published, with the Latin or Greek on one side and the Catalan on the other; Hemingway appeared in Catalan before he was ever translated into Castilian Spanish. The language is close to Provençal in form and structure, and is spoken quite far into France; in Spain it has two distinct dialects — Majorcan and Valencian. In the plays of the eighteenth-century Catalan writer Robreño, the gentry in the cast spoke the more effete Castilian Spanish, whereas the low life mocked them in a wonderfully picaresque Catalan; in the late nineteenth century, Catalan literature was far more distinguished than Castilian. (In a broad sense, Castilian Spanish imposes its formality on

[113]

the speaker, whereas in Catalan the speaker dominates the language, which varies from person to person.) Since a healthy unofficial language smacks of separatism, the central government has tried at various times to suppress the official appearance of Catalan — in 1916, for example, it refused to deliver letters in Catalonia if the names of towns and streets appeared in their Catalan spelling — but in 1932, when Catalonia gained its autonomy, Catalan naturally became an official language, and Catalan writers looked forward to a firmer future. The Franco regime, however, has set about systematically to suppress it once more. The teaching of Catalan was and still is prohibited; it remains very difficult to secure official permission to publish anything in Catalan; radio programs and plays in Catalan are expressly forbidden; and the Catalans complain that, with the steady migration into Barcelona of workers from the rest of Spain, spoken Catalan is losing its purity.

During the decade following the end of the Civil War, the regime was conspicuously successful in putting a damper on the arts in Catalonia, and at that time, with the Spanish-French frontier tightly closed, any contact with the rest of Europe was impossible. The lid, however, did not stay down. In Barcelona, I managed to borrow some copies of a defunct local magazine that now has some fame — a frail publication called the *Dau al Set* (Catalan for "the seventh face of the dice"), which came into being in 1948 and lasted spasmodically for four years. It was started quite spontaneously by a small group of writers and painters, and more or less took its form from their regular meetings and conversations. "We were all very gloomy at the time," one of them explained to me, "belonging as we did to that unfortunate generation that was too young to fight in the Civil War but old enough to remember it almost too vividly. I recall how my mother used to weep uncontrollably for days on end, and that memory still shakes me. In 1948, we began to talk and talk, all of us desperate, aware that we had to find *something* to do, something to let off our steam. We were hungry for anything at all — we discovered the Surrealists and Sartre and jazz and Romanesque art all at the same time, and we went mad." The magazine was a just reflection of this madness — I found in it a poem in Catalan called "Blues for One Day on Which St. Francis of Assisi Wanted Also To Be a Negro" — but it was amazingly inventive and energetic, and even though it had to be printed clandestinely and circulated to a limited group of subscribers, it set in motion a whole generation of writers and painters. The painters, at least, have gone on to gain a great deal of international attention and personal success. ("There's no point these days in fighting bulls or going into business," I heard one Spaniard say. "If you're too fat to be a footballer, be an abstract painter.") The writers' problems do not arise for the painters, and their work has become a recognizably valuable commodity in that most recent branch of investment banking, the international art market.

Catalonia is rich in painters, painting, and the sudden physical astonishments that provoke them — Picasso spent eight early, impressionable years in Barcelona, which is now honoring him with a small museum; Dali returns loyally to the Costa Brava; and Miró, though he now lives on Majorca, was born in Catalonia and in spirit never left it — and currently it is enjoying a new abstract abundance.

In Barcelona, I visited Antonio Tàpies, one of the original *Dau al Set* group and a painter who commands considerable respect among other painters. Quiet and soft-spoken, he was utterly disinclined to talk about painting; we spoke of the censorship. "For us, the problem scarcely exists," he said, "though it can crop up now and again in the matter of titles.

I had some difficulty over a painting I was sending to New York, which I had called 'Opposition,' and I had to defend my title as an aesthetic statement. But since the censor is so stupidly capricious over the matter of books, what can he be expected to do with abstract painting? No, we painters are in a very odd position; our work is drawing a lot of attention to Spain abroad, and the government actually encourages us to send paintings to exhibitions all over the place, but at the same time, since we are artists, it doesn't quite trust us. We are very, very lucky, though, compared to writers. When we were putting out *Dau al Set*, the writers opened my eyes to so much, and yet they are still stuck in the same corner, hardly able to breathe."

Later on, the subject changed, and Tàpies became very emphatic about his roots in Barcelona. "I was born here, and I live between the city and a house I have in the country," he said. "When I take — as I must — two or three trips a year, to New York or Paris, I get increasingly jumpy as time passes, and I hurry back. I never get used to Barcelona, and I still spend much of my time walking about in it. It has a physical tingle, something that for a painter is quite tangibly important. In my work, I depend utterly on its *ambiente*. I could not work in Madrid, that *theoretical* city. But look what we have here — we have the Mediterranean, and we have Gaudí."

I grew to appreciate both of these elements, as they swam regularly across my vision. In the middle of the city, you are hardly aware of the sea, but if you climb to its upper reaches, the sea stops you in astonishment — smoky blue, spreading lazily away into the hazy distance, deservedly legendary. Near the harbor, you can doze away the better part of a day in the sheer shimmer and tang of it. Tied to the quay at the foot of the Ramblas is a clumsy replica of Columbus's *Santa María*, built some ten years ago for a movie. For five pesetas, you can go aboard. The sailor in charge will show you his washing and try to sell you a pamphlet, without enthusiasm. For eighteen pesetas, you can do a tour of the whole harbor, past the curious, square mussel-fishing hulls and the ships waiting to go to the Canaries or New York or somewhere. But if you choose to dawdle all day on the steps, in the daze of the sun, as somebody always seems to be doing, nobody will mind.

As for Gaudí, he was an architect who made a mystique out of *Mediterraneanismo*, a theory to the effect that the angle of light in the Mediterranean was the only proper light for showing off architecture. The theory was a typical extravagance; the light, as he knew better than anybody else, is a perpetual wonder.

Gaudí is the presiding genius of the city. Even after you know where they are, his buildings lie in wait for you and stop you. I had seen them all before — I had gone to Gaudí exhibitions, read books on him, looked at photographs, talked about him — but, coming across these creations day after day in the context of the city, I began to see them all in the fifth dimension of amazement, looking as if they had suddenly occurred like momentous mushrooms — a kind of wild architectural laughter. Gaudí belongs completely to Barcelona. He was born Antoni Gaudí i Cornet in the Catalan town of Reus, in 1852, studied architecture at the Escuela Superior in Barcelona, and practiced it faithfully in and around the city, which he seldom left, for over fifty years, and where he died in 1926, a few days after being knocked down by a streetcar on his way to church. Even though he did not have in his lifetime anything like the towering reputation he has now, he had something more immediately satisfying — the passionate attention and even devotion of the people he lived among, and in particular the whole-hearted backing of a few wealthy and influential families, who more or less gave him his head. And an incredible head it was, brilliantly inventive and original from a technical point of view, wildly visionary, and unquenchably imaginative; he was half mystic, half social idealist, something of a saint, and everything of a genius. His exuberant working life coincided with a time when Barcelona was bursting out all over; new industries were starting up and expanding, the working classes were replacing the creaky feudalism of the past with a flood of political idealism, and the cultural revival, or the *Renaixença,* as it was called in Catalan, was in full cry. *Art nouveau* raged, and Gaudí was its prophet, though he was too tumultuous and original to be confined by any style. He plundered the medieval and the High Victorian Gothic; he copied forms directly from natural objects; and he used indigenous Spanish craftsmanship to the full in his ceramics, in his stained glass, in the wrought iron he scribbled across his buildings like a personal handwriting. Most of all, he made all his whirling elements cohere in a series of local buildings that, whether they are considered monuments or eyesores or simply marvels, are bound to astonish by the fact that they are there at all.

Gaudí's most famous building is the Expiatory Temple of the Holy Family, a project he undertook in 1883 and worked on steadily for the rest of his life. He became so passionately absorbed in his work that at one time, when a lack of funds seemed likely to curb its progress, he went out daily to beg for funds in the street. Enough donations did come in (the cathedral was to expiate the sins of the industrial age) to bring it to its present stage; although it has no interior — only the crypt, the east wall, and the great south door, with its four fanciful spires, are completed — it has at least acquired its proportions, and can easily be completed in the imagination. Work still goes on (a good deal of time went into repairing it after the workers tried unsuccessfully to raze it in 1936, when they pillaged and destroyed Barcelona's sixty-odd churches), but it is still financed by donations. Mr. Evelyn Waugh has suggested that perhaps a millionaire slightly wrong in the head might put up the funds to finish it — a suggestion that fills me with dread, for while the times abound in millionaires wrong in the head, the Sagrada Familia, towering dizzily up to its brightly tiled pinnacles, stands at present as the most impressive modern ruin we have. One day as I was walking past it, I saw a small boy dribbling a red football across where the nave would be, ant-sized under the cascades of finely carved stone. I felt that Gaudí would have been delighted at the sight.

As becomes a genius, Gaudí was thoroughly eccentric. A Catalan to the fingertips, he refused to speak Castilian, and he would move all over the city on foot, scorning comfort, often attended by a flock of young architects, who hung on his pronouncements. No Catalan remains indifferent to him, and even the people who dismiss him and his period do so with a suspicious vehemence. Gaudí spanned an extraordinary epoch; while he was building the Palacio Güell, he designed a circular ramp for horses to descend from the street entrance to the stables under the house, and in the same lifetime he made designs for the interior of a cinema. On two occasions, I climbed to the Parque Güell, on the rising heights of the city — a park he built and landscaped on part of the estate of the Güell family, rich textile manufacturers who were his principal patrons. When Don Eusebio Güell died, the city took it over and opened it as a public park. It is a favorite haunt of children, full of fanciful gardens, cascades of colored tile, miniature castles, wandering walls, mazes of irregular columns, waterfalls and flower beds, close to the vegetable wonderland of Alice, the stone rooted like trees, the trees stony in appearance. A notice warned me not to roller-skate, but I would never have dreamed of it; roller skates are as out of place in Gaudí's world as clockwork animals would be in the jungle. The best thing about the Parque Güell is the obvious pleasure children take in it. A small girl was perched on the back of a green-and-white tile turtle, obviously enchanted at finding a world that corresponded remotely to the forms and colors of her imagination; I would not have been surprised if she had broken off a corner of the iridescent castle and eaten it. Far below, the Mediterranean winked away. A workman lay asleep in the hollow of a great blue eye in the wall, his arm flung over his eyes. What an awakening he would have, I thought.

Years ago, when I was coming to Spain for the first time, I had a conversation with a friend in London who had passed a large part of his life in Spain, had fought in the Civil War, and had afterward been forced to return to England. I often recall it. "It is dangerously easy for a foreigner to grow extremely sentimental about Spain," he warned me. "To go there, especially from the North, is a thorough liberation — you have the steady, healing sun, which simplifies life considerably, and you have an abundance of humor and sheer joy. As a foreigner, too, you can accept all that greedily, without having to take on any of the responsibilities. To me, Spain and Ireland are the last two human countries left, where sheer human crankiness manages to resist all the forces of order and efficiency, where the fact of being alive at all is held as a cause for celebration. If you were ruthless enough, you might be able to live off that easily available joy for long enough, but I think that eventually you will find yourself beginning to despair, as I did. When you discover the price that Spaniards pay for choosing to retain an utter human anarchy, you will despair of it even more, perhaps, than they do. A country that rests so heavily on its past, expecting miracles to happen simply because they always have, creates for itself, these days, an impossible present, and the greater the frustrations that Spaniards suffer in trying to achieve some form of social organization, the further they retreat into their personal contexts. The sun, the pleasure of the moment become for them a refuge from doom. But you cannot take the responsibility for them. All you can do is see clearly. Spain is theirs, not yours."

The meaning of this, as happens with most wise conclusions, has dawned on me slowly; I have, with time, gone through the stages my friend described — the ready and frequent delight, the frustration, the despair, and, ultimately, the belief in miracles. The most peculiar characteristic of the Spanish *ambiente* is that in taking any long view of the disastrous past or the inconceivable future, Spaniards trap themselves so tragically in their own paradoxes that they must at once reach for the only tolerable reality available to them, the living moment. In a sense, their relief at finding themselves alive at all transforms the moment into a miracle at hand — the seat in the sun, the wine on the table, the shrug, the release of laughter. Some of them manage to live entirely in that ever-extending moment; others are given over utterly to despair. Between these extremes lie all the varieties of the Spanish temper.

With all this, a foreigner in Spain is in a particularly vulnerable position, unless he goes there blandly and unabashedly because of the sun or the low prices and manages to keep his eyes fixed on his navel. Although a stranger has no responsibility for the condition of Spain, he is made to feel it more acutely than the Spaniards themselves do, since, unlike them, he is not confined to a particular class or situation; sometimes in the span of a single day he may talk with a plumber, a clutch of painters, a pomposity of businessmen, all of whom will be only too ready to explain Spain to him, so that he ends up with an armful of attitudes and compromises, and a sense of the whole denied to his various informants. Bit by bit, he reaches logical conclusions, only to find that none of them apply, since the problem is not his in the first place. If he ventures to advance them, Spaniards pounce on him gleefully. "Ah, but you are not a Spaniard!" they exclaim. "How can you understand?" Since in Spain everybody is a separate instance, or a *caso*, as they say, the contradictions thicken and tangle, and one takes one's seat in the sun with near-Spanish relief.

While I was in Barcelona, the regime of Generalísimo Franco arrived at what was for it a moment of quivering importance — the twenty-fifth anniversary of Franco's nomination, on October 1, 1936, as head of the Spanish state. For the occasion, the Generalísimo travelled to the Castilian town of Burgos, where the title had been conferred on him, trailed by all the available television and radio apparatus in the country (a fact that annoyed the people of Barcelona more than any other, since it prohibited the televising of the football match between Barcelona and Madrid, which took place in Madrid the same weekend). To watch the jamboree at Burgos, I went to a small, flyblown bar by the harbor, a favorite haunt of mine for some years because of its buoyant clientele. Recently, it has prospered enough to buy a television set, not for daily use but for special occasions; then, as on that afternoon, it is wheeled out, uncovered, dusted, and switched on. Deprived of the football game, the Sunday regulars had decided instead to turn to the proceedings in Burgos, wavering between disgust and curiosity. By the time I joined them, the Generalísimo had warmed up, looking for all the world like an elderly aunt on her hundredth birthday, astonished by the turnout of relatives at her bedside. A popular Catalan poem circulating in Barcelona about the Generalísimo lays the finger of poetic accuracy on him:

> *The relentlessness of the Cid,*
> *The authoritarianism of Philip II,*
> *The will to power of Charles V,*
> *And the voice and backside of Isabel la Católica.*

The high-pitched voice was the only one in the bar, and faces watched the set a bit sheepishly, finding it perhaps difficult to believe that the dapper little figure on the screen could have any connection with the sins committed in his name. But as the implacable bombast unrolled, they first began to gawk in disbelief and then to hoot with laughter.

"There is ample room within the broad ideals of our Movement for all Spaniards who, in their private, professional, and family lives, respond generously to the daily call for sacrifice for our native land," piped the Generalísimo.

"For you, little Paco, I give up eating meat," muttered a small man beside me.

"There is always room in prison, even for the fattest," growled another.

"Spain must begin to march to the rhythm of the new Europe, live in tune with the economic and social progress of the world, but at the same time it has to preserve unmolested its political stability and its national independence," the Leader was saying.

"Cha-cha-cha," said the small man.

"His wife wrote that," added his friend, "so that she can buy her pearls in Paris."

"My words at this time are words of well-deserved gratitude to all Spaniards who, in the activities of our nation, have been those who have directed the fundamental advance of our regime, who have given a lead to the generation that will follow — a lead in political thought, in intellectual life, in daily work," Franco went on.

"He's speaking about us," said the little man. "He likes us. He's our friend."

"Why don't you kiss him then?" replied the other.

The little man's reply does not translate easily into English.

Sitting in the darkest corner of the bar was an enormous man whom I had seen there quite often and whom I knew well enough to nod to. His face creased up like a relief map, his jowls shook when he laughed, his quick black eyes missed nothing; over his black sash a great belly bulged. The others called him El Cínico (The Cynic). When he spoke, as he did now, the glasses rattled.

"You all make me sick," he said. "If you don't like little Paco, why don't you turn him off? You're still free to do that, you know. Or why haven't you turned him off, good and proper, years ago? I'll tell you why — because then you'd have to think instead of just grumbling, and if this whole dust heap of a country depended on the fruits of your mosquito brains, we wouldn't even have sitdown toilets. Call little Paco all the names you want, but at least he's taken the weight off *your* backs. What if he does put a few of us in prison? If I were where he is, I'd have the lot of you inside in a shake, for all the good you do. Take a look at Paco." El Cínico waved his huge arm, and eyes flickered to the screen, where the Generalísimo was waving his arms. "All he's doing is talking. And all you do is talk, talk, talk, until you make me sick. And if you think that's nonsense, what he's saying, I'll tell you that it's nothing to the nonsense and slop I've listened to in this bar, dribbling out day after day."

The others, used to him, were laughing and moving away. Someone switched off the set, and the waiter replaced the cover and the vase of flowers. But El Cínico would not be stopped. He glared around him. "All right, I'm a cynic," he said. "But at least I'm honest. I don't pretend that the little wart will disappear in smoke, and that the churches will fall down and the jails empty. We'll have a nastier face and a squeakier voice, most likely. Don't argue with me. Look at you — Catholics till you're twenty, Communists till you're forty, then Franco's friends because you can't think of anything else to be. Join my party — come on. We drink and we spit. But at least we're not sorry for ourselves because we let all this happen, and we're not above taking the blame."

He looked as though he might rant as long as the Generalísimo. I waved to him and left.

Even El Cínico gave the proceedings at Burgos more attention than most; the following morning I watched men break open their newspapers, pass over the laudatory headlines without a glance, and turn to the sports pages. The majority of the people have accepted the twenty-five-year-old facts that political responsibility is no more than a theoretical notion, and one that can have nothing to do with the realities of Spanish life; that the instances of censorship and social injustice usually happen to others; that Franco has kept things together after all; that talking gets nowhere; and that life goes on. Somewhere under the surface there is a longing for action of some kind, any kind — a longing that languishes with the passing of time but that might still explode into violence. Yet the appetite grows less, and the aspirations are muted.

Most political conversations in Spain are like variations on a worn-out theme, but when I talked once or twice with some university students in Barcelona I was relieved to find that, far from indulging themselves in fashionable apathy, they were extremely down-to-earth, hardheaded, even brutal. "Look!" one of them said. "Franco is sixty-nine; I am twenty-two. You can understand that I don't waste any time on him, or on the past, since, sure as eggs, I'll survive him. As far as we're concerned — those of us who care, and we're not very many, because most of the students are busy looking for a comfortable niche in the city — Franco has got away with doing nothing at all for twenty-five years, in which time Spain could have been coaxed into the twentieth century, could have been made fruitful and productive. One of these days — it doesn't matter when — we'll inherit the wreckage, and we're going to have to do something with it, something direct and practical. I spent three years studying law — that used to be the thing, to take a law degree — but then, after thinking about it, I decided that I couldn't be anything of a lawyer under the regime, so I switched to economics, as did most of my friends. Facts are what matter to us — facts and a real situation. You see, we grew up overhearing the fruitless arguments of our fathers over why the Republic failed, and I think we turned by instinct away from all political theory, for our concerns are not political at all. Whatever follows Franco — the monarchy, a military junta, a republic, or Communism — it can waste no time in facing the fact that economically Spain is on the bottom, and it will have to get busy at once with things like agrarian reform, irrigation, building, and new industry. We believe Spain can be brought to its feet not by American aid but by work and intelligent planning, and to that end we're involved in just finding out the facts. At the same time, we care very much that the country should keep its essential human character and not get sucked into the same sort of materialism as America and now Europe. That's perhaps wishful. But we don't want Spain to go on being a kind of circus act, all flamenco and wineskins. We want it to become a serious, working country, with the people behind it, and we see all kinds of ways of bringing that about — ways that Franco has ignored through fear of losing power. Power politics are old-fashioned; work is not. You know well enough that the tragedy and frustration of Spaniards is that, with all the will in the world, they are given no room to act, nothing to do but look at their own long, tragic faces in the mirror — until they can stand it no longer and break the mirror. Well, we don't look in the mirror; we look out of the window."

The current of life in Spain is punctuated by anniversaries — fiestas national and local, saints' days, days on which, for ritual or private reasons, this or that shop may close and telephones never answer. For two or three years, the government has been trying to reorganize the Spanish working day, to eliminate the afternoon siesta and the evening hours. Some private offices have acquiesced and others have reacted contrarily, with the result that Barcelona's working hours are in complete anarchy. One day, I had lunch with three friends who calculated that, officially, they were only entitled to fifteen minutes together; the lunch, however, lasted a good two hours. With the Feast of the Merced safely over, and the overtones of Franco's silver wedding at Burgos frittering out, I expected a period of steady normality, in which one day might follow another according to a sensible plan. But I was caught; going out one Thursday, I found the shops shuttered up tight, the traffic sparse, the walkers dressed up, the children with bows in their hair, the cafés overflowing. Not until I bought a paper did I learn that I had stumbled into Columbus Day, celebrated in Spain as the Día de la Raza — the Day of the Race, or the Day of Spanishness, when thoughts, according to the editorials, are meant to turn to the momentousness of the Spanish race, past, present, and future. In fact, they were turning gleefully to food, drink, and diversion.

The newspaper was full of woolly eulogy, with messages from His Excellency the Chief of State and from the Holy Father, a re-creation of the discovery of America, and a rash of notes on Columbus, who is another of Barcelona's distinguished shades. A huge cast-iron statue of him stands at the foot of the Ramblas, dominating the harbor; he bestrides a great orb, a scroll in his left hand, his right arm outflung, pointing in the general direction of the New World. A rickety elevator takes tourists and the curious up into the orb itself for a panorama of the harbor. (Two men managed to station themselves in the orb during the day of the rising in 1936, accompanied by a machine gun and a plentiful supply of ammunition, with which they sprayed the Ramblas and the harbor until nightfall.) It was to Barcelona that Columbus returned in March, 1493, to bring the news of his discoveries in person to Ferdinand and Isabella, who were there with the court, and where, fêted and decorated, Columbus "rode at the King's bridle." The association does not stop there. I discovered a small knot of scholars and addicts in Barcelona who have gone a long way toward proving, at least to their own satisfaction, that, far from having been a Genoese, as the standard history books have it, Columbus was in fact a Catalan, and that his Spanish name, Colón, was actually an emendation of "Colom," a not uncommon Catalan name. (The situation is thoroughly confused by the frequency with which Columbus changed his spots and his name in order to find favor and financial sanctuary with this or that reigning monarch; he became Colombo to please the Portuguese, and Colón to satisfy Ferdinand and Isabella.) I was beginning to warm to the subject, with the help of a fat primer published in Barcelona and entitled "Colón Tal Cual Fué," or "The Real Columbus," when I went to call on the publisher of the book, José Porter, a distinguished local bookseller and the champion of the Columbus-was-a-Catalan set. He received me in his overflowing bookshop, sat me down, and presented me with the salient points of his argument at top speed, jumping up and down as he did so, and jabbing in my direction with his cigar for emphasis.

"I can't really tell you the whole story now," he cried. "It would take days, and besides, I'm writing a book myself that I venture to say will put the question beyond all doubt — once, finally, and for all, period. And I don't want to let the cat out of the bag quite yet. The idea that Colón came from Genoa is one of those notions that somebody once brought up and that stuck, without any real evidence to support it. If he was a Genoese, why didn't he write in Italian? Why do we have hundreds of his letters in Castilian Spanish and none in Italian? It's all nonsense, all nonsense. You can take it from me that Colón was born not in Genoa at all but on the island called Genova, at the mouth of the Ebro, just out from Tortosa, in Catalonia. In fact, a hundred and fifty kilometers from this very city. Of *course* he was a Catalan" — the cigar jerked in my direction — "and, what's more, the card he wrote from the Canary Islands, the card that bore the first news of the discovery of the New World, was written not in Castilian but in Catalan. No copy of it now exists, but in the catalogue of Colón's library, the bulk of which went to his illegitimate son Fernando and was housed in Seville, there exists the handwritten entry referring to this very letter, with the note 'written in Catalan.' He was born

[129]

Juan Colom, not Cristobal Colón, but he suppressed his Catalan origin so as to find favor with Isabella and make sure of the wealth of Castile as backing for his voyage. And there's plenty more evidence, but for the moment it will have to wait, because it's time for me to close up the store. But read my book when it comes out; you'll see I'm not talking nonsense. Juan Colom, remember, a *Catalan!*"

We shook hands, and I went out into the street, ready to do battle with the first Genoese who crossed my path, in the name of Juan Colom and Señor Porter.

I passed a lamplighter, lighting the lamps with a flame, although we were on a busy enough business street — "plunk," they went as the wick caught. My way home took me past the Church of San Felipe Neri, the church to which Gaudí used to walk to Mass every day from his studio beside the Sagrada Familia. (Barcelona once boasted an Avenida Gaudí, but it is now the Avenida General Sanjurjo. It would be worth someone's while to make a study of the changes in street names in modern Spain; most of them now have a military cast, and read like a roll call of the Nationalist Army. They will be changed again soon enough, and when they are, Gaudí is sure to get his avenue back.) It was on one of these walks that the old man was knocked down by the streetcar; when he died, a few days later, the whole city mourned him, and a campaign was started to keep the traffic under stricter control. Now, thirty-five years later, the traffic is wilder than anyone then dreamed it could be. The yellow taxis swish past, the drivers gesticulating, and the occasional donkey carts look like forlorn lifeboats in the sea of cars. I was wondering what Gaudí would have made of the giant neon excrescences in the Plaza de Cataluña, when somebody clapped me on the shoulder. It was a Catalan poet whom I knew, and he was waving a letter at me. We sat down

at a café, starting up a flurry of waiters, and before I could begin to tell him about Columbus he pushed the letter into my
hand, explaining it to me as I read it.

"It's a terrible thing to happen to me, of all people," he
shouted above the traffic. "I've been offered a job, and I'm supposed to go to London. London!" he almost screamed, and it
occurred to me, there and then, that "London" was, in fact, a
very ugly phonetic assemblage. "Why, tell me, do they pick on
me? I write quiet poems; I've never demonstrated in public, or
shown traces of ambition. And *this* arrives." He flicked the letter with his fingernail.

"Just a minute," I said. "You don't want the job?"

"Of course I don't want it, man! I'd like the money, naturally,
but if I have to go there, then it's just not worth it. They think
they're giving me a present of London, whereas, as I see it, all
they're doing is taking Barcelona away from me. Well, I won't
go, and that's an end of it."

"Oh, come on," I said. "It won't hurt you."

He looked at me dangerously. "You think it doesn't matter,
because you travel all over the place," he said. "And I grant you
that there are plenty of sound arguments for getting out of a
place like this, a city where you can still be fined for kissing in
the streets. But for me, Barcelona has all I ever want to see and
feel, all within walking distance. If I'm out of it for a day, I
begin to think that something terrible must have happened,
that all my friends must be looking for me. In London, I'd pine;
I'd grow thin with longing, and probably die of grief. Don't try
to convince me. Just order me a glass of beer."

"Think of Juan Colom," I said feebly, because I was on his
side. "Travel is said to broaden the mind."

"Colom!" he snorted. "Today I discovered a new *tasca,* and I
go on discovering and rediscovering Barcelona, street by street,

[131]

stone by stone. There must be plenty of people in London already. All I want is to stay here."

The beer arrived, and he raised his glass to me.

"As for my mind, it's as broad as Barcelona, and that's broad enough," he said gravely. "Anyway, about travel, I don't think it does anything at all. Travel, my friend, means only a change of flies."

III

Foreigners

Owls, like monks of a rare, feathered order,
haunt one aloof, lopped tower in this
unlikely city, cresting the broken stones
like ghosts at dusk, watchful, wary,
describing soft, slow curves in the failing sky.

Supremely odd and patiently oblivious
to all but wind and owlhood, they tatter
the evening air with their broad, sooty wings.
And over all, the tower seems content
with its alien colony. For whose is a city?

Yet below, the jabbering birds of the sprawled suburbs
complain from the lower roofs, look up from crusts
and blame owls for the dust, for all the dismal
workaday winging. The atmosphere is crowded,
to their native eyes, with a woeful weight of owls.

Natural enough, their twitterings. They were there
first, they cleared the air and made
nests in new places, scraped for straws, foraged
for food, grew ancestors and histories.
Now come the owls, a late, impervious entry.

What do the owls answer? To wit, nothing.
And sure enough, with time passing, the tower
becomes a landmark, mentioned in the guidebooks,
with owls as appropriate appendages. The city
absorbs them into its anonymous air.

Now, other birds alight on the battlements,
occasionally singing. Not worthwhile to war
over a lack of crumbs, in alien weather.
Who gives a hoot, say owls. The wind is common.
Let all poor birds be brothers under the feather.

Disguises

My selves, my presences,
like uniforms and suits,
some stiff, some soiled, some threadbare,
and not all easy-fitting,
hang somewhere in the house.

A friend or a misfortune
will force me, on occasion,
into a sober habit,
uncomfortably formal,
in keeping, though unwise.

But otherwise I wear
something old and easy,
with little thought to please,
nor a glance in the mirror,
nor a care for size;

being caught, in consequence,
sporting the wrong color
in inappropriate weather —
odd shirts, uneven socks,
and most unsuitable ties.

I should have a tailor,
or, failing him, a mirror;
but being possessed of neither,
I sit in my stubborn skin and count
all clothing as disguise.

Speaking a Foreign Language

How clumsy on the tongue, these acquired idioms,
after the innuendoes of our own. How far
we are from foreigners, what faith
we rest in one sentence, hoping a smile will follow
on the appropriate face, always wallowing
between what we long to say and what we can,
trusting the phrase is suitable to the occasion,
the accent passable, the smile real,
always asking the traveller's fearful question —
* what is being lost in translation?*

Something, to be sure. And yet, to hear
the stumbling of foreign friends, how little we care
for the wreckage of word or tense. How endearing they are,
and how our speech reaches out, like a helping hand,
or limps in sympathy. Easy to understand,
through the tangle of language, the heart behind
groping toward us — to make the translation of
* syntax into love.*

The Syntax of Seasons

Autumn was adjectival. I recall
a gray, dank, gnarled spell
when all wore fall-quality, a bare
mutating atmosphere.

Winter hardened into nouns. Withdrawn
in lamplight, I would crown
the cold with thought-exactitude, would claim
the drear air with a name.

In spring, all language loosened and became
less in demand, limping, lame,
faced with the bursting days. What told
was tongue-tied wonder at the green and gold.

Steeped now in summer, though our chattering
rises and falls, occasional as birdsong,
we fall to silence under the burning sun,
and feel the great verbs run.

The Figures on the Frieze

Darkness wears off, and, dawning into light,
they find themselves unmagically together.
He sees the stains of morning in her face.
She shivers, distant in his bitter weather.

Diminishing of legend sets him brooding.
Great goddess-figures conjured from his book
blur what he sees with bafflement of wishing.
Sulky, she feels his fierce, accusing look.

Familiar as her own, his body's landscape
seems harsh and dull to her habitual eyes.
Mystery leaves, and, mercilessly flying,
the blind fiends come, emboldened by her cries.

Avoiding simple reach of hand for hand
(which would surrender pride) by noon they stand
withdrawn from touch, reproachfully alone,
small in each other's eyes, tall in their own.

Wild with their misery, they entangle now
in baffling agonies of why and how.
Afternoon glimmers, and they wound anew,
flesh, nerve, bone, gristle in each other's view.

"What have you done to me?" From each proud heart,
new phantoms walk in the deceiving air.
As the light fails, each is consumed apart,
he by his ogre vision, she by her fire.

When night falls, out of a despair of daylight,
they strike the lying attitudes of love,
and through the perturbations of their bodies,
each feels the amazing, murderous legends move.

Outlook, Uncertain

No season
brings conclusion.

Each year,
through heartache, nightmare,

true loves alter,
marriages falter,

and lovers illumine
the antique design,

apart, together,
foolish as weather,

right as rain,
sure as ruin.

Must you, then, and I
adjust the whole sky

over every morning;
or else, submitting

to cloud and storm;
enact the same

lugubrious ending,
new lives pending?

Me to You

Summer's gone brown, and, with it,
our wanderings in the shires, our ways.
Look at us now.
A shuttered house drips in Moroccan rain.
A mill sits ghostly in the green of France.
Beaches are empty now of all but pebbles.
But still, at crossroads, in senorial gardens,
we meet, sleep, wrangle, part, meet, part,
making a lodging of the heart.

Now that the sea begins to dull with winter,
and I so far, and you so far,
(and home further than either),
write me a long letter,
as if from home.

        Tell me about the snowfalls
at night, and tell me how we'd sit in firelight,
hearing dogs huff in sleep, hearing the geese
hiss in the barn, hearing the horse clop home.
Say how the waterfall sounds, and how the weeds
trail in the slithering river.
Write me about the weather.

Perhaps
a letter across water,
something like this, but better,
would almost take us strangely
closer to home.

Write, and I'll come.

IV

VI

Drows

WHEN the first English rural stationmaster, whoever he was, bored with the drab formality of his station name-plate, decided to spell it out in seashells or twigs or even begonias, he cannot have realized then that, even in his innocence, he was one of the unwitting ancestors of a curious race that has multiplied alarmingly since his day, an obsessed and bug-eyed coterie bent on beating us over the head with the observation that words, while they may have a sound and a connotation, have also an appearance, and that this appearance, wherever possible, should be made to underline the meaning or, better still, *be* the meaning. I am just as keen as anyone that words should look graceful and appropriate in their place, and that a page of type should be well-balanced and readable. But to this small band of revivifiers, this is only a beginning. Their dearest wish appears to be that words should not only speak to us but more, that they should rush and throw their arms round us, fetch our slippers, and act out their meanings like small, portable charades.

I can take some of this, in moderation. I think I must have managed a faint smile the first time I read, on a billboard, the word LOOK with eyes instead of O's. But when ICICLE never turns up without a glacier cap reminiscent of the Matterhorn, all I can hope for is a quick thaw. I like the word "icicle" well enough unadorned, and my imagination is quite capable of turning it efficiently into a short mental documentary of winter. The same goes for the other animated favorites. I don't have to have the word BOMB blowing up in my face, or STRETCH drawn out agonizingly across the page. I may be unnecessarily obstinate; but I cannot honestly feel that printing RED in actual red gives my imagination any extra kick. If anything, it makes it sulk. And now, when designers, through some perverse subtlety, are likely to print the word RED in bright blue, my imagination just goes home and pulls the covers over its head.

Oh, the abhorrent horrors of the visual alphabet, jumping up and down, shouting at us from the posters! — I's that are cigarettes or candles, G's that are golliwogs, O's that are wheels, balloons or pennies, L's that are £'s, S's that are $'s, words that split and shiver and disintegrate in our faces. Tedium, tedium, tee dee um tum tum. I'd like to catch the infant genius who spawned the gray, out-of-focus job which, after I had blinked and peered, I discovered to be saying SUFFERING FROM EYESTRAIN? Of course I was, by then; I hope he went blind. And I'd also like to send a picked band of junior thugs after the man who perpetrated the poster face with its moustache already meticulously pencilled in. I have a recent bitter loathing for furniture in fields and beds made in meadows. But these are by the way, like cars in bedrooms and dinner tables on the open sea, and all the other ludicrous whimsies of the visual astonishers.

Where language is concerned, however, there is a serious point to be made. Language is language, words-on-a-page, and since ever it has been agreed on as the most intricate and subtle form of human expression, it has been transcending its own cramped limitations in a quite masterful manner, by verbal invention, by device and artifice, by sheer magic. A typesetter cannot do very much for the poems of Coleridge beyond giving them a graceful look, and making them appear as clear and honest as they are. If he fancied himself enough to design the title and text of the *Ode to Melancholy* so that they drooped and writhed in the spirit of the poem, or chose to print Edward Young's *Night Thoughts* in black on a black page, he would be hurried out of business. Painters who from time to time have tried to transcend the two-dimensional limitations of a canvas by making three-dimensional paintings have learned mournfully that limitation is the stuff of art. If words were to prove more *effectively communicative* (the phrase is borrowed from designers) by getting up and dancing, as words occasionally do in certain misguided film-animations, then they would long ago have ceased to be words and instead would have come to live among us, a new race of tiny little antlike creatures, a small and hyper-communicative chorus-line of meaning, a living, breathing Braille.

The more one learns to marvel at the sinewy possibilities in the pure use of language, the less inclined one is to clutter it up with appendages even as innocently occasional as the exclamation mark, let alone to countenance words bursting into graphic flames, or letters standing on their heads. A designer would probably claim that the assemblage SDRAWKCAB conveys its meaning more succinctly than BACKWARDS; but he would quite simply be wrong. Nor does neon do anything more for a word than make it readable at night. If I were told in quiet type to drink a pint of milk a day, instead of being chanted at in colored pidgin Italian, I would be much less resistant to the idea. It is understandable that the happy hunting ground of designers should be amongst the monosyllabics of advertising, where words seldom have to convey more than a grunt or a gasp, an OOOH or an AAAH. Words chosen to be carved in stone are, for the most part, suitably sombre; things written in blood are required to be grave. But what can be spelt out in silk stockings, chocolate or assorted foodstuffs except something suitably inane? Whoever first said that a photograph was worth a thousand (or was it a hundred?) words was making a grave mistake. Photographs are photographs and words are words, and no comparison seems conceivable to me. But when designers jump in and begin photographing words scratched in sand, or the like, then confusion might understandably arise.

Dear design — if we dare leave the word in simple type, uncolored, unphotographed, undressed — is still in its brawling infancy, which means that, as it approaches the difficult years of its adolescence, we may expect to see words running visually wild — aeroplanes writing SMOKE in the sky, ties which say TIE all over themselves, legions of children forming the word OOOH! on a mile-long chocolate bar, photographed from a helicopter, and eventually, at design's coming-out party, a great multicolored firework display which goes off and blurts the word FIREWORKS into the night.

Palindromes

TALKING, writing, using words is a kind of behavior; and, as with all kinds of behavior, it has its quirky, odd side. I confess to an unnatural affection for the word "context"; and I think I must use "periphery" more than anyone else living, partly out of the feeling that it is an underdog among words, and partly for the pleasure of saying it. These are small aberrations. But there are people who cherish all forms of abbreviation, and who speak a kind of shorthand; there are people who pronounce capital letters, who lisp in an affected babytalk, who underline with their voices, who stud their speech with superfluous French, who first-name everything from kings to plays. Be these as they may — affectations, mannerisms, annoyances; what I am talking about is more profoundly odd and personal — the peculiar word-behavior which hangs over from childhood, perverse pronunciations, school expressions, favorite family misspellings, personal metatheses and the like. (One of my sisters had a doll called Betty Copyright. Her name was imprinted on the sole of one foot.)

My own predilection, which began with the dawning of words in my consciousness, was to read everything backwards. I don't know how or why it started — I may have wanted language to lead me back to the womb; but Brownies in one of my childhood texts became Seinworbs to my backward mind. At this time, I was busy discovering words, poring over the labels of sauce bottles to extract every drop of relish from the word-assemblages — *puhctek* had me in thrall, particularly *otamot puhctek.* I wandered amazed past shops and billboards. Wonders like *muelonil* and *ffuns* unfolded before my eyes. I drove my father half-mad one summer by referring to him as *rehtaf* for months on end. I set the household on its ear by insisting on calling the dog *God.*

All the reasons for this obsession probably do not bear examination. I only know that the habit has persisted, and that I read on theatre marquees strange gnomic riddles like *im er od,* and *Notca* and *Enobelyram* on the *dnuorgrednu.* It may not be evidence of a go-ahead life; but it does add an extra dimension to the process of being born and dying, and has led me into some absorbing *srenroc.* I suppose one of the turning points was my discovery of *OXO* on a billboard. It had me coming and going, and it made a memorable impact. Somewhere in the recesses of the language were a few rare words which ran both ways, and I began to ferret them out with a loving zeal — *eye, eve* and *level,* and then *minim* and *refer.* Even odder, *reward* and *repaid* changed their skin completely in the other direction; and when I reversed *live,* I could hardly contain myself. It was a short step from there to my discovery of the palindrome, and when I came on *Madam, I'm Adam* in a dictionary of my father's, I was hooked, to use a neologism.

I don't know what the palindrome demonstrates. It must be easily the most useless assemblage of words in the language, since it makes no more than an abstruse technical point, and its substance is conspicuously inane. But how thrilling it is. *Able was I ere I saw Elba* carries no illumination, and Napoleon was certainly innocent of its utterance; but it is firmly lodged in the head of every ex-schoolboy. For poets especially, palindromes are weirdly fascinating. (Scratch a poet and you find a latent crossword-puzzler, an acrostic and word-game addict, a maker and breaker of codes and ciphers; anything new to be wrung out of the manipulation of words is meat and drink to him. In its purely verbal aspect, poetry is a kind of applied Scrabble.) In my case, I knew I would never rest until I had added a palindrome to the language, and my unconscious over the years kept busy riffling through word lists in the wrong direction, preparing the ground. Palindromes are not by any means confined to English. Latin has the line *Roma tibi subito motibus ibit amor* for a start. Spanish seems only to have one, *Dabale arroz a la zorra el abad,* as inane as they come. French is richer; Louise de Vilmorin recently published a clutch of them, neatest amongst them being *Eh, ça va, la vache?* The longest palindrome in English is reputedly: *Dog as a devil deified deified lived as a God,* a fairly unsatisfactory example, to my mind. My imagination has always sneered at it.

From time to time, on a Sunday or a wet day, we would embark on palindromes; but they generally frittered out in feeble flubs like *Step on no pets* or *Ragusa sugar, aha, ragusa sugar!,* examples best forgotten. The most serious palindromist in English was Thurber, who applied himself assiduously to the genre, and produced *Peel's lager on red rum did murder no regal sleep,* an advertisement disguised as a line from Macbeth. His greatest palindrome, *A man, a plan, a canal — Panama,* deserves to be enshrined on a monument since, for once, besides fulfilling its difficult technical requirements, it rings with true acclaim.

One day about a year ago, I awoke with the word *gnat* plying backward and forward in my mind; and I felt that my moment had arrived. I sat down at my desk with a proper sense of destiny. (Palindromes bear no resemblance to any other form of writing. For one thing, they have to be worked from both ends simultaneously, and the moment of truth comes when the two halves meet in the middle and have to be joined in such a way as to complete the sense as well as the design.) Fortune and my rich past served me well, however, and after three hours, I was able to utter a small croak of triumph. I make no great claims for the result. It contains no illumination, but it is formidably long.

T. Eliot, top bard, notes putrid tang emanating, is sad. I'd assign it a name: "Gnat dirt upset on drab pot toilet."

The dream which preoccupies the tortuous mind of every palindromist is that somewhere within the confines of the language lurks the Great Palindrome, a nutshell which not only fulfills the intricate demands of the art, flowing sweetly in both directions, but which also contains the Final Truth of Things. The few palindromists I know mention this wistfully, hopefully. But to discover it — would that not be a noble work of man?

The World of Z

THE letter Z was a latecomer to the alphabet, more of a
gatepost than a door, one of the alphabetical staff rather
than an active member, severe, structural, emphatic and final.
What A begins with awesome amplitude, Z finishes sharply
and firmly — *zip zip zip,* a matter of three straight lines. It was
not, in fact, until the fourteenth century that Z won a firm
place on the team — prior to that, it sat stiffly on the bench,
liable to be called in for severity's sake, where S seemed too
soft and sibilant. The letter hung about the English dialects
under a variety of names — *izzard, ezod, uzzard* and *zad* — and
even after it was admitted in the end, it kept a dual identity
— *zee* in the United States, *zed* in England — an oddness which
divides the English-speaking world as emphatically as does the
Atlantic Ocean. Looking under Z in the dictionary, one dis-

covers that, by the time it gained official status, the other letters had had the pickings, and fewer than two hundred words, most of them technical, could be scraped together to give Z a little more to do initially than simply close and lock the book.

Mathematics, however, sponsored the new letter, since Z stood for the third unknown quantity, after X and Y; but Mr. Z never attained the social prominence of Mr. X. As a sop, Z was given zero and the zenith to look after, both appropriate extremities. But beyond that, the decisive, buzz-saw sound of the letter earned it a function in its own right, and when the zip-fastener was invented, Z was the obvious candidate to take it over. A "sipper" would have seemed both silly and wrong. Z also gave the proper pazazz to zeal and zest, although zest originally meant the touch of lemon peel added to a dish. Z is beloved of carpenters, who lean heavily on the Z-bar to join and fortify three planks of wood. Open window shutters in France say Z Z Z Z, all over the housefront. "Zounds," a euphemism for God's wounds, is out of fashion as an oath; but the zodiac is likely to keep Z to the fore for a long time, not to mention the ever-present zeitgeist, Zionism, and — the letter's latest acquisition — Zen, the monosyllabic philosophy of harmony and delight which antedated beatniks and abstract painters, and will long outlast them.

The world of the letter Z is a bizarre one, zany, amazing, and puzzlingly miscellaneous, a world in which gongoozlers gawk at assorted wonders, amongst them zulus, zombies and jazz, coins like the zloty and the zwanziger, and a whole zoo of irregular creatures, the zebra, the zubr, the buzzard, the zaratan, and, not least, the ziczac, an Egyptian plover whose main function is to warn his unlikely friend, the crocodile, of approaching danger, ziczac ziczac. Zigzags are something else, and what letter could better explain them than Z, a roadsign in itself? Zigzags, however, are not confined to roads — Jane Austen mentions "the little zigzags of embarrassment," and an English parliamentarian recently warned us to keep a keen eye on "the zigzags of international negotiation."

Z has its heroes — Zeus, who, whether as bull or swan or man or god, enforced his rampant male will on Olympus and toppled the sovereignty of the female; Zarathrustra, or Zoroaster, who spake in black and white; Azazel, the angel of despair; that whiz, the Wizard of Oz; Zoilus, a Greek literary critic, the first to give Homer a bad review, whose carping manner has carried over; the geometrical Aztecs; and Sergeant Buzfuz, who still hazes the courtroom with rhetoric. Not too admirable a gathering, perhaps, but one in which all the protagonists made their marks sharply, *zip zip zip.* Z people are critics rather than creators, more concerned with structure than substance, cool, sharp and attentive, ready to put an abrupt end to the wandering of words, specialists who prefer the background, but who nevertheless hold the sprawling mass tightly together, and who are likely to break out into unpredictable, unerring laughter.

The world of Z buzzes like an air terminal, an outpost from which the alphabet takes off into silence, or like a dizzy bazaar festooned with fez and lizard, where ends meet. Ending anything is difficult. Neither X nor Y were able to round out the alphabet emphatically enough, and so it ultimately fell to the crispness of Z. "Time to take a zizz," says the Englishman after lunch; and as the Z Z Z's flow steadily out of his sleeping head, the rest, indeed, is silence.

The O-filler

One noon in the library, I watched a man —
imagine! — filling in O's, a little, rumpled
nobody of a man, who licked his stub of pencil
and leaned over every O with a loving care,
shading it neatly, exactly to its edges,
until the open pages
were pocked and dotted with solid O's, like villages
and capitals on a map. And yet, so peppered,
somehow the book looked lived in and complete.

That whole afternoon, as the light outside softened,
and the library groaned woodenly,
he worked and worked, his O-so-patient shading
descending like an eyelid over each open O
for page after page. Not once did he miss one,
or hover even a moment over an a,
or an e *or a* p *or a* g *— Only the O's —*
oodles of O's, O's multitudinous, O's manifold,
O's italic and roman.
And what light on his crumpled face when he discovered —
as I supposed — odd words like zoo *and* ooze,
polo, oolong *and* odontology!

Think now. In that limitless library,
all round the steep-shelved walls, bulging in their bindings,
books stood, waiting. Heaven knows how many
he had so far filled, but no matter, there still were
uncountable volumes of O-laden prose, and odes

with inflated capital O's (in the manner of Shelley),
O-bearing Bibles and biographies,
even whole sections devoted to O alone,
all his for the filling. Glory, glory, glory!
How lovely and open and endless the world must have seemed
  to him,
how utterly clear-cut! Think of it. A pencil
was all he needed. Life was one wide O.

Anyway, why in the end should O's not be closed
as eyes are? I envied him. After all,
sitting across from him, had I accomplished
anything as firm as he had, or as fruitful?
What could I show? A handful of scrawled lines,
an afternoon yawned and wondered away,
and a growing realization that in time
even my scribbled words would come
under his grubby thumb, and the blinds be drawn
on all my O's. And only this thought for comfort —
that when he comes to this poem, a proper joy
may amaze his wizened face, and, O, a pure pleasure
make his meticulous pencil quiver.

The World of Q

Q IS emphatically the oddest letter in our alphabet, less sociably co-operative than the others, separate, distinct, self-sustaining. Above all, Q is the letter of awe and wonder, the restless letter of question and curiosity, the oblique letter that accommodates and characterizes the rarest qualities, from quaintness to queenliness, a graceful wry twist of a letter, open-eyed yet with its tongue in its cheek, a letter that deserves to be the badge of the odd, the very quiddity and quintessence of being human.

In the ancient Irish Tree Alphabet, Q derived from Quert, the wild apple tree, the repository of mystery, under which the elusive White Hind hid her head; in most Indo-European languages, Q is the letter of interrogation. Latin asks persistently in Q's — *qui, quo, quando, quomodo, quis, qua, quot, quare;*

and although English has softened the Q-sound to a gentler *wh*, or occasionally to a *cu*, under every *who, which, what* or *why* a Q is lurking. The question-mark itself is undoubtedly a formalization of the letter Q, the equivalent of a raised eyebrow or a rising inflection. But what is even more significant is that the formal, rational, painstaking, categorical Greeks suppressed the letter κοππα and became Q-less. Their questions were *pi* ones — πον, πωs, ποθεν, etc. Even their question-mark was a curt semi-colon. For them, the mystery could not be left alone — it had to be explained away. In Greek, the letter Q would have looked out of place, much too round and humorous and irregular. A similar difference existed amongst the Celts, the P-Celts and Q-Celts who settled in Pritania or Qritania, the P-Celts more adaptable, docile and orderly, more quickly absorbed by the process of civilization, the older Q-Celts more stubbornly resistent to it, wilder, more oddly poetic. Whatever the origins of the mysterious expression, *minding one's P's and Q's* — and the explanations abound, from pints and quarts to printer's devils — its implications are clear. The spirit of P is clarity itself, pure, logical, aloof and cold; the spirit of Q continues quirky, poetic, cranky and warm. The two letters jostle one another in the alphabet, in uneasy proximity.

The world of the letter Q, for all its quicksands, quarries and quagmires, is a small, rare one, more preoccupied with quality than quantity, a tiny island of wit in all dictionaries and directories, a world in which questions always supersede answers, where there are quips enough to keep everything a-quiver, where quidnuncs counter any tendency towards stultification, where a contrary quirkiness constantly opposes itself to the stiffness of theory.

Q counts amongst its heroes and touchstones a bizarre assortment — the noble, knobbly knight Don Quixote, the wry master of questing; Peter Quince the carpenter; the poet Quarles ("Judge not the play before the play is done"); the Marquis of Queensberry; Falstaff's Mrs. Quickly; the hunchback Quasimodo, and a pride of Queens; places as farflung as Quebec, Quincy and Loch Quoich; creatures as curious as the quail, the quagga, and Lear's Quangle Wangle Quee; the Quantum Theory, quartz and quicksilver; and the quince, the love-emblem of Aphrodite. The Isle of Man is a Q-island, where oddities abound and odd things happen, where Q-names clutter the telephone book:

> Quilliam Quirk was a Manxman bold,
> Three cork heads and a crown of gold.

It may be no accident that Q is absent from the telephone dial or that it should be the favorite monosyllable of waitresses and bus-conductors, the quintessence of politeness; or that the obsolete interjection, *Quoz*, introduced into the language through a hoax played by a Dublin theatre manager called Daly, can still express a healthy and independent disbelief.

Among Q-people, quests still count, qualms are still felt, wise words are occasionally scrawled with quills, looks are quizzical, and nights are quilted. Q-people quibble away, and are still capable of being astonished by the quirkiness of things. Q-people, after all, prefer the quick to the dead. *Q.E.D.*

V

V

Tell Us Where to Go,
Guv'nor, and We'll Go

As a people, the English like nothing more than to have their national conscience pricked as regularly as possible. Waifs and underdogs are meat and drink to them; lost causes give them a pleasure akin to that which cats must take from having their fur rubbed the wrong way. This pricking of the conscience is a service that is performed with alacrity by the more rampant of the English popular newspapers, which boil daily with indignation and manage to whip their readers into a perpetual frenzy over a variety of causes and crusades, domestic and international. In a country as parochial as England, not all the smoke is without fire. I found this out when I gave my attention to the sad lot of the English gypsies, or "travellers," as they have always preferred to call themselves — an itinerant and ancestral segment of the population of the United Kingdom that for some time has been gradually reaching the end of the line.

The "gypsy question" was dumped unceremoniously in the country's lap on December 1, 1961, when, in the House of Commons, Mr. Norman N. Dodds, the Honourable Member for Erith and Crayford, a constituency in Kent, rose to put the following motion before his fellows:

> That this House, recognizing that the loyalty to this country of the Romany people and other travellers is in no way inferior to that of any other section of the community, is of the opinion that Her Majesty's Government in coöperation with local authorities must devise and implement, as a matter of urgency, a national policy which will insure adequate living quarters for the gypsies and other travellers, and provide for their good health, proper education, and full employment.

Following his motion, Mr. Dodds warned the House that he would make a long speech, and though — being a blunt, outspoken, and eminently practical Northerner — he was as good as his word, the House listened with a profound and dumbstruck attention as, for two hours, he laid before it the bare bones of a situation which, in the weeks that followed, caused a good number of Englishmen to open their eyes wide. "Of course, we'd all known there *were* gypsies," one Member of Parliament told me. "I remember them in ones and twos and families, but I'd never before thought of them as a *minority group*. Somehow, it never occurred to me to think of gypsies as a part of society at all, since they are always on the periphery."

The essential import of Mr. Dodds's speech in the Commons was that the gypsies, who for upward of four hundred years

had lived a travelling life in tents and caravans, taking spas-
modic seasonal employment and camping in various sites that
they used by tradition, if not by right, had recently fallen foul
of the times, and, in the name of progress, had been hounded
from many of their old encampments by the police, acting on
the orders of local town councils. Since the end of the Second
World War, Britain has been expanding, first at a trot and
latterly at a gallop, and housing developments, and even new
towns, have been springing up across the countryside, leaving
England considerably less green and pleasant than it once was,
and causing local councils to give much more thought to the
uses and abuses of the common land under their jurisdiction
than they once did. Among honest householders, gypsies have
a bad name simply because, without necessarily being dis-
honest, they have never chosen to be honest householders; local
councils, faced with a steady series of individual complaints
about gypsy encampments, have been solving the problem
simply by serving notice on the gypsies to get moving, under
pain of fine or imprisonment. Where they were to move *to* was
nobody's responsibility. The situation was further complicated
when, in 1960, the Government passed the Caravan Sites and
Control of Development Act, an ordinance designed to restrain
the arbitrary parking of caravans and trailers — mainly by
holiday-makers — on any sites other than those appointed for
the purpose and provided with water and proper sanitation.
Not only were gypsies unpopular on the camping sites but, in
the wake of the Act, even those individual farmers who were
well disposed to the gypsies and in the past had set aside a
corner of their land for the gypsy caravans were no longer
allowed by law to do so. "But where can the gypsies go?" one
anxious landowner asked her local magistrate. "Legally, nowhere," was his reply.

[167]

After the House debate, the newspapers and weeklies took up Mr. Dodds's cause, and gypsies were suddenly given the center of the stage — a spot that their whole tradition and way of life had carefully shunned. Some of them were dragooned into appearing before the television cameras, and from others the newspapers managed to extract a few terse remarks — "It don't seem right to us, Guv'nor, now, do it?" In any event, the problem came across to the public, and the *Economist* of December 9, 1961, put a cool finger on it:

> Thanks to successive Town and Country Planning Acts, which gave local authorities draconian powers to close down so many of their caravan sites as eyesores, Britain's persecution of its gypsies is now mortifyingly worse than the treatment of them in most totalitarian countries. . . .
> The loss of nearly all their traditional camping sites and the failure of their traditional crafts in modern England have practically destroyed the George Borrow type of gypsy life to which Augustus John became so attached. There is no sense in trying to remake that life artificially; but neither is there any excuse for hounding a minority tribe of vagrant people out of their traditional ways and occupations (and, in the end, out of existence).

Mr. Dodds's carefully documented speech — he demonstrated effectively that almost every other country in Europe had made better provisions for its gypsy population than Britain had — was suddenly thrown into sharp relief when a cluster of over ninety gypsy families living in Darenth Woods, near Dartford, in Kent, was suddenly served with an eviction notice. On January 20th, 1962, early in the morning, a group of policemen arrived at the camp, looking appropriately sheepish, and proceeded to tow away the caravans. The gypsies themselves went quietly, and the caravans were left in a dangerously exposed position by the side of a trunk road — where, incidentally, they constituted a contravention of the Highways Act. The chairman of the local council claimed that he was only acting in accordance with the expressed complaints of local citizens, and that the ultimate fate of the gypsies could not be his concern. The incident was agonizingly reported in the popular press, and the comments of the local taxpayers were fairly typical of a strong body of feeling in rural England toward the gypsies: "Well, they used to steal children, and I wouldn't want my nippers to end up in a caravan." "They're dirty, they never wash, and the woods are full of junk." "They steal anything — anyway, whether they do or not, I can't get to sleep for feeling they might." "They don't pay any taxes — why should they have any rights at all?" "We would leave them alone, but they'd never leave us alone — always bringing junk to the door, or just plain begging. Far better to get rid of them altogether." "I wouldn't want my children to play with their children, and learn all those filthy words."

What proved so tantalizing to everyone who began to take notice of the gypsies was not only the absence of facts and figures about them but the almost impossible difficulty of ascertaining these — the gypsies have no idea how many they are, simply because they have never needed to know, or thought to care. One of Mr. Dodds's principal objectives was to persuade the government to set about taking a census of gypsies and travellers in the country, for, as he pointed out, he had been able to find no accurate account of their numbers except in a report published in Helsinki in 1901 by one Arthur Thesleff, which put the gypsy population of the British Isles at twenty thousand. He himself guessed the present figure to be close to a hundred thousand, but, as has since become clear, nobody has any accurate idea. Various local attempts to take stock have always been complicated by the fact that the gypsies, unpredictably on the move, either got themselves counted several times over or didn't get counted at all. Also, inevitably, fierce argument has always arisen over the sticky question of authenticity. Are all travellers gypsies? Can vagrants who take to a wandering life on the fringes of the civilized world for reasons that do not always bear examination be counted as travellers, or ought they to be prosecuted for vagrancy? Should not some distinction be made between true Romany gypsies, who are a blood race, and *diddikais*, or half-castes, who have forfeited the purity of their tradition and are using gypsydom as a way of escaping responsibilities? And if so, is it possible to tell — or, more difficult, to verify — which gypsies are true Romanies? It is easy to imagine the precise bureaucratic mind boggling at it all.

The gypsies are elusive enough to baffle anyone, statistician or no, and since they have remained illiterate, they have kept no record of themselves beyond the bizarre reaches of their own inventive memories. Nor are they at all astonished at themselves.

"A gennelman come 'ere one day and said as we is all from India," one old gypsy woman told me. "So I says to him, 'Well, maybe we is, Surr, but it don't make a mighty difference, now do it, Surr?'"

Most of the scholarly investigation into their origins has been forced to proceed through the medium of the Romany language, and while there has been some inspired guessing, the history that has been re-created is mainly a suppositional one. Britain is an outpost of gypsydom, one of the last stops in the spread of the travellers across Europe; in modern times, the largest concentration of Romany gypsies was to be found in Hungary and the Balkans, and it was there that a group of Hungarian and German scholars discovered, toward the end of the eighteenth century, that many Romany root words were suspiciously close to the Aryan languages of India, which had their origins in Sanskrit. They were able to be even more precise in tracing the gypsies' exodus from India, for the linguistic evidence showed that it must have been before the evolution of modern Hindustani, with its Arabic infiltrations — a linguistic event that is dated at approximately A.D. 1000. The supposition is that the gypsies migrated gradually to Europe by way of Byzantium; at any rate, by the fourteenth century they were thickly ensconced on the Balkan Peninsula, and from there they spread slowly across Europe, becoming, variously, atzigan, zingari, zingani, tzigani, zigeuner, cigani, cygani, gitanos, and gypsies. No one quite knows (a qualification that should probably precede every statement about them, to the point of monotony) when they first arrived in the British Isles, but early in the sixteenth century references to them begin to turn up in Scotland, then a sovereign country separate from England. In 1530, James V, the reigning king of Scotland, paid them to dance before him at Holyrood Palace, in Edinburgh, and ten years later he concluded a most magnanimous agreement with "our loved John Faw, Lord and Earl of Little Egypt," granting extraordinary privileges to the "Egyptians," as they were called. (There are many explanations for this appellation, but the most likely one seems to me that the Scots, who took their Scriptures literally, regarded these travelling strangers as incarnations of the prophecy of Ezekiel: "I will scatter the Egyptians among the nations, and will disperse them through the countries." Certainly the theory that they might have come from Egypt is, I have found, a cause for scholarly scorn.) In England, however, the Egyptians did not fare so well, and apparently made such a conspicuous nuisance of

themselves that Henry VIII had an act passed as a warning
to them:

Afore this tyme dyverse and many outlandysshe People callynge
themselfes Egyptians usyng no crafte nor faicte of marchaundyse
have comen into this Realme, and gone from Shire to Shire and
Place to Place in greate company, and used greate subtyll and
crafty meanes to deceyve the people, beryng them in hande, that
they by Palmestre coulde telle menne and womens fortunes, and
so many tymes by crafte and subtyltie have deceyved the people
of theyr money, and also hath comytted many and haynous felonyes
and robberies to the greate hurte and deceyte of the people that
they have comyn amonge . . . from hensforth no such persones
be suffred to come within this the Kynges Realm.

The gypsies obviously ran against Henry's grain, but he was
certainly not alone in his judgment of them, for in the sixteenth and seventeenth centuries gypsies were the victims of
fear and suspicion all over Europe. The belief that they practiced the black arts and stole children led to the most proscriptive measures being taken against them, and since they
were an incoming minority, they were made scapegoats for
all forms of shadowy double-dealing — as, in a sense, they still
are.

It would be silly to imagine that the suspicions arose without
cause. In 1608, Thomas Dekker observed wryly:

Their apparel is odd and fantastic, though it be never so full of
rents; the men wear scarves of calico, or any other base stuff, hanging their bodies like Morris-dancers, with bells and other toys, to
entice the country folk to flock about them, and to wonder at their
fooleries. . . .

Yet the simple country folk will come running out of their houses
to gaze upon them, whilst in the meantime one steals into the next
room, and brings away whatsoever he can lay hold on. . . .

They (forsooth) can tell fortunes; which for the most part are infallibly true, by reason that they work upon rules which are grounded upon certainty: for one of them will tell you that you shall shortly have some evil luck fall upon you, and within half an hour after you shall find your pocket picked or your purse cut.

Since from the beginning the gypsies were never given any inducement to become solid citizens, however, it is hard to tell which is the cause and which the effect.

Although deportations were frequent during the eighteenth century — in 1715 a small group of gypsies was transported from Scotland to the Colony of Virginia — the active persecution of the gypsies appears to have dwindled considerably by the time the century ended, despite the fact that vast numbers of them were pressed into service during the American War of Independence. The fear of persecution remained with them, however, even though they were more or less left alone to follow their traditional crafts, to work seasonally at fruit- and hop-picking, and to mind their own rural business.

For an account of the full range of the gypsies' activities (and, indeed, for whatever information does exist on the traditional English gypsy life), I am indebted to the *Journal* of the Gypsy Lore Society, a small band of enthusiasts who, from 1888 on, have published a series of monographs that brim with the kind of detail that is otherwise lacking. The *Journal* lists a hundred and thirty-five distinct kinds of work undertaken by gypsies, but in the main they appear to have taken on any form of work that was occasional and that fitted in with their travelling habits — they odd-jobbed for farmers in almost any capacity; they cut clothespins and wove baskets; they had an uncanny way with animals — particularly horses — and their disorders; they told fortunes and practiced herb medicine; and they danced and sang. Beyond that, they were dealers to a man, which meant that they occupied themselves in acquiring anything at all, provided that it could be acquired for nothing and sold for something — a sound enough principle on at least the lower slopes of economics. "Can you read and write?" asks a kindly visitor. "No, Surr, but we kin count, and that's what do matter, now ain't it, Surr?"

England has always had its staunch gypsophiles — notably George Borrow and Augustus John — who tended to use the gypsies in the manner of authors in search of characters, but now that the gypsies have been given the stage as a serious social problem, these romantic preoccupations have been discredited. Mr. John Wells, the Member of Parliament for Maidstone, waved Borrow aside in the House of Commons debate as having "done more harm to the cause of those of us who wish the gypsy community well than almost anything else." This is probably unfair, since we owe practically all of what we know of the gypsies to people who, like Borrow, took the trouble to live with them, get to know them, and keep some clear account of their life. "We are like the cuckoo — everyone speaks ill of us, but nobody would wish us away," Borrow quotes one old gypsy as saying, and the remark is a fairly romantic gloss of the truth, even though it is not exactly subscribed to by local councillors in present-day England. What is quite true is that those who have "gone with" the gypsies have almost always done so out of a romantic dissatisfaction. One group of gypsies with whom I recently spent some time told me with great glee of a woman who came to visit them regularly, bringing them presents and aspiring to the travelling life. "Imagine her!" said one of the men. "She wanted us t' go on outside on a cold winter's night and make us a fire and all sit round about it, Surr, and us all supposed t' sing, with our teeth chatterin', an' all. Let her come an' stay in this here cara-

[174]

van an' let all of us be goin' t' stay in her house in London is what I say to that!" Another told me, "It be all right for the likes of them. They comes an' sees us — and they is good to us, mind you, Surr — but then they goes on home again, and it's us who stays. And it's us as the police wants t' move on, not them." There was no bitterness — only an inability to understand how anyone could want to be a traveller who was not born to it. "They asks us if we wants t' be travellers, and we tells 'em 'tis not as if we wants t' be or no — we was born travellers, and we *is* travellers."

What anyone who goes patiently in search of the gypsies discovers — and what a good number of newspapermen and television interviewers have had to learn, to the point of dumfoundment — is that gypsies react strangely to questions, and, in fact, are always on their guard with any but their own people. Since in the past they have mostly been questioned belligerently by some form of authority, they appear curiously evasive, but the truth is that most of the time they either have understood the question imperfectly or have strained to give the kind of answer they felt the questioner wanted from them. Partly for that reason, many of the conversations they appear to carry on have an odd, irrelevant cast. In London, I was lucky enough to come across Mr. William Larmour, a small, keen-eyed Northern Irishman who, as a Methodist missionary, had worked among the gypsies in Hampshire and on the outskirts of London for more than thirty years. He knew a vast number of gypsy families by name, and they, in their turn, held him in great esteem and talked openly to him. In the course of my conversation with him, I found out a great deal about gypsies; as for the gypsies themselves, they told me that he was one *gorgio* (their word for a non-gypsy) whom they felt they could treat as one of their own.

[175]

"I myself have not much patience with the theories and notions about the gypsies," Mr. Larmour told me. "They're nearly always based on some very queer preconceptions that are simply not true. To me, the gypsies are just like children; they tell you lies as children do, not to deceive you but to try to wish something true. And on top of that, they've never been treated well. They've always been blamed for things whether they did them or not, they've always been looked on suspiciously, and they're cowed, as animals can be cowed. That's what has made them so secretive — the feeling that everybody's down on them. When I first went among them, in the hop fields in Hampshire, I used to talk to them for long stretches, until it dawned on me that while they went on nodding and smiling, they weren't understanding a word I was saying. So I've always talked to them since as I would to children — slowly and patiently, making sure they had got hold of one thing before I went on to the next. I remember once on Epsom Downs, when I was talking to them on the text 'God is our refuge,' I asked them if they knew what a refuge was. None of them did, so I explained it to them by saying that if you went after a rabbit, it ran away into its hole, and the hole was a refuge for the rabbit. A little while later, when I came back to it, I asked them again what a refuge was. 'I know, Surr,' said one. 'It's a rabbit hole.' What you have to understand is that the travellers have always been illiterate, and this means they cannot grasp abstract ideas. They only understand particulars, and their minds connect in a curious way, in terms of what they have either experienced or been told — nothing more. For that reason, they've never been able to argue their own case, or even claim rights to which they are entitled, unless somebody helps them. At the same time, that has drawn them closer together. Family loyalty is very strong among the travellers. They like to stay together, and depend very much on one another. As for their being crafty, there's no doubt about their having an eye for a bargain, but if you have nothing to begin with, it's quite natural to be preoccupied with getting something for nothing. They're fine people, if you take the trouble to understand them — loyal and faithful, with a great natural sweetness to them. And if they're suspicious of *gorgios,* all I can say is, well they might be."

I asked him about the present trouble, and he spoke quite vehemently.

"Oh, it's bad, all right. You take Hampshire, where they always went in large numbers for the hop-picking — and they were good workers, mind you. Well, nowadays there are machines to pick the hops, for one thing, and with odd work less sure than it once was, the travellers have begun to think more about settling in one place. Also, you can't make much of a living from cutting clothespins in these days of automatic spin dryers. It's foolish to say the travellers don't want to live in houses — most of them would, if they had a chance of steady work. And the biggest change of all will come when the children go to school regularly and learn to read and write — they're very quick, you know. When that happens, in a generation or two, the travellers will blend in with the rest of us. Travelling isn't the easygoing thing it was once, what with the high cost of living and so many people. There's no room now, and I think most of the travellers will jump at the chance to get ahead. But they'll never turn against their gypsy blood; I haven't met one who wasn't proud of it, to himself."

I wanted to know what Mr. Larmour thought about distinguishing between real gypsies and other travellers.

"Well," he said, "there's been an awful lot of nonsense talked about that, I can tell you. I've heard plenty of people claim they could tell by looking, but they don't have any idea. The pure Romany gypsies are fewer than they were, yes. And I doubt whether you could even find one who spoke Romany and nothing else. Nowadays Romany is much more like a spare vocabulary, a private family language. But I don't like this notion of *real* — I don't like anybody talking about a real Irishman, or a real anything else. To me, the real gypsies are the ones who have stayed faithful to the travelling life and tried to live it as honorably as they could, staying out of trouble, keeping to themselves. It's the *false* ones that should be picked out, if you like — the no-goods who have used the gypsies as a cover and have given them a bad name. The gypsies don't have any time for them, either. As for whether any gypsy is a real gypsy or not, you'd do better to take a gypsy's word for it. They know who is one of them and who isn't. And if they're not always sure, you can bet that no local councillor or police constable is any more able to tell than they are."

The more I talked to gypsies, the more grateful I was for Mr. Larmour's clear eye; I learned to listen instead of talking, to avoid asking questions, and to follow their curious conversational wanderings. As we sat in the caravans, which were always scrubbed and polished, and contained a small shrine of family photographs, the members of the family would come in, one by one, and stand around, watching; then, slowly, they would unbend and begin to talk among themselves, and I would withdraw and listen. The talk almost always centered on travellers and the travelling life and the hazards of making a living, and the speakers often switched bewilderingly between the present and the past, reaching back into the recesses of the family to find, it seemed to me, some kind of anchor in time. I also came across plenty of the irrelevance that Mr. Larmour had mentioned. One day, while I was eating bread

[178]

and cheese in one of the caravans, I mentioned how good the cheese tasted, and a little man in the corner, who had not previously spoken, started up at once. "I mind of a man in Hampshire," he said, "and one day when he were mendin' the wheel of his wagon, the wheel upped and run away, and so he run after it, for miles it was, and by the time he catched it, so beat was he that he says to the wheel, 'You just go on back, and I'll come after,' well, that man, *he* liked cheese." Jumps like this were quite common; nobody attempted to keep any control over the conversation, or seemed to be going anywhere; words were as arbitrary as natural events, as unpredictable as weather. Romany words cropped up now and again, but the gypsies themselves were the first to tell me how much the language had declined, and how far they themselves were from using it as easily as their parents did. "We *rokker* it now when we wants to say something a *gorgio* shouldna be hearing," said one of the men. "And we uses it for the names of things, for the likes of our *vardos* and our *groys;* it wouldna seem right to us to call them wagons and horses. But nowadays, Surr, the youngsters don't even know the words no more, and when they get goin' to the schools, well, you won't hear no word of Romany, for we is the last ones to have it, and it will sure enough die when we does. Same as the long frocks and the old four-wheeled *vardos* and the *dukkerin* [fortune-telling]. But it don't make me sad no more. Me, I'll *make* 'em go to school, so as they may read all them books to me, and we shall all find a bit o' work in a steady place, and we won't do no travellin' no more. And maybe it's time, Surr. It ain't what it were, the travelling life. I'd be for takin' a house or a steady site, if it come my way, and I don't mind a bit o' rent, either. We shall have to mend ourselves a bit, yes — less *slicker* [garbage] round the camp, the boys workin' steady, a bit o' money tucked away, different ways to what we is used to. I would not be speakin' a word against the travellin', only the winters is cruel, and the people they makes it rough nowadays, and the police they moves you on and maybe takes a fine from you, and you never knows as where you can set down — now, that's no livin', Surr, ain't it not?"

More than the men, however, the gypsy women resent the present, and their own inevitable transition, for they have always seen themselves as the guardians of gypsy manners and traditions. It was the gypsy women who held the families together, and at the same time *dukkerin* was their own art — something that they still speak of with the utmost awe and secrecy. One evening in the country, I came across a fine old woman who the others had told me was *divio* — a Romany word that means something between crazy and enchanted. Straight-backed and clear-eyed, she was taking in her washing, and she invited me into the caravan to get warm. Unlike the other gypsies I had met and listened to, she was neither resigned nor cowed nor wistful over the ups and downs of her changing times; instead, she was magnificently arrogant and full of scorn.

"I tell you what, Surr," she said, "they don't have no idea of what it be, gypsyin'. It were our life and our breath, and we knew we was *special* folk, not just anyone's poor animals. Us Lees, we was always famous for the *dukkerin*, because we *knowed*. As a young girl, I could tell from a look who were *bokky* [lucky]. I just *knowed*. Many's the time I been *dukkerin* in the shires, and we was respected for it, and we was let be. Changed it has, Surr — not just us Romanies but the *gorgios*. There be no room in this world, not for us nor them. I tell you now I never goes out *dukkerin*, because I don't have no heart for it — there's none left as understands them things, Surr, and

I wouldna waste my *rokker* to tell 'em such as they do not want to be hearin'. So I just goes out an' I gives 'em a bit o' the palm now and again, but what I sees I keeps to myself. I knows our ways is goin', Surr, but I is proud o' the blood, Surr, and I knows it be a sad world that do not let us go *dukkerin* in it, for fear of our telling, us who never asked no more than a corner to be left quiet in."

One of the peculiar traits of the English gypsies has been their inclination to localize themselves — to wander, yes, but only along certain beaten paths, in a fixed, seasonal round. I noticed that in conversation they referred to themselves as "Bucks people" or "Dorset people," even though their wanderings almost always took them to Hampshire in the summer; they were neither curious nor eager to extend their range. When I spoke to them about the French or Spanish gypsies, they feigned interest at first, and then shook their heads. "They would not be knowin' us, Surr, unless we was connected in the family. There be a heap o' travellers we never talks to, neither — *diddikais,* tinkers, an' all. We is private folks, Surr."

This stirred me up a bit, for my own sharpest memories of the travellers were of the tinkers in the Highlands of Scotland, and though their life approximated to that of the English Romanies — except, perhaps, that it was considerably less decorative — the gypsies I talked to would not hear a good word about them. "Chancy folk, them tinkers," they told me. "You never knows as where they is going." I did not exactly take the gypsies' word for this; since I was on my way to Scotland, I hoped to find out for myself.

In its treatment of the travellers, as in almost every other exercise of human judgment, Scotland has always differed markedly from England, possibly because the Scots, by nature, are more appreciative of human oddity and have never approached the same point of conformity that modern England has. My childhood in Scotland was thick with "characters"; looking back on it, I cannot see that any norm existed. As a result, the tinkers there must have found the going a good bit less difficult, at least on the psychological level. Two very distinct strains of travellers settled, or wandered, in Scotland — the tinkers, or tinklers, who were of Celtic origin and who infiltrated into the west of Scotland from Ireland, and the Romany gypsies, who came north in the early sixteenth century and confined themselves to the south. The Romanies, who are known as "muggers" in the Border country, converged on a small village, Kirk Yetholm, about a mile from the English border (in the past a very convenient spot, since fugitives from either English or Scottish justice could flit up or down the hillside and disappear over the border within a matter of minutes), and the village gained a lasting reputation as the gypsy capital of Scotland. More records remain of the Yetholm community than of any other gypsy settlement in Britain, and this came about mainly through the humanitarian foresight of a minister of the parish, Dr. John Baird, who in 1838 formed a Society for the Reformation of Gypsies in Scotland. In one of his reports, Dr. Baird predicted that schooling, steady employment, and marriage outside the gypsy community would eventually blur the edges of their separateness, and this he set out to achieve, with "his purse and his door always open," according to a contemporary account. The Faas, or Faws, the first gypsy family in Scotland, lived in Yetholm, and in 1861 great numbers of travellers gathered there to celebrate the coronation of their last queen, Esther Faa Blyth, who could "read a man's soul in his face" and was fond of saying that she needed fifty faces herself — a face for the minister, a face for a gentleman, a face for an honest man, a face for a scoundrel, and so on. She was visited by Queen Victoria and George Borrow, and she threw her support behind the policies of Dr. Baird and encouraged her followers to take up steady work — with some success, I discovered when I went to Yetholm on a bleak, snowy March afternoon, for one of the leading gyspy families now runs a conspicuously successful road-haulage business there. The minister of the neighboring parish told me he had once had the last of the Faas as his church beadle. "Fine-looking man," he said, "and no more eccentric than the rest of us here." One curious fact about the Yetholm gypsies is that as they settled, the Romany language that they originally spoke declined to a few popular words, used by natives and gypsies alike. I even found a few of them lurking in the recesses of my own vocabulary.

The point about Dr. John Baird is that he did, in essence, what Mr. Dodds and the more responsible elements in English journalism are trying to get done now, except that he managed to do it directly, without bureaucratic confusion, and in a time and place where overcrowding and overcivilization were unlikely prospects. He also managed to make the Scots much more conscious that they had in their midst a travelling population; they took a regular census of the travellers, for one thing, and they were more inclined to let their travellers be, perhaps because Scotland is, if anything, underpopulated and there is a good deal more free ground for encampments and for wandering.

The tinkers, however, are quite another matter. For one thing, they are very much older than the gypsies in point of occupancy, descending as they do from the wandering smiths of ancient Ireland. For another, they are Celts, and so are less alien to the native population; as Lewis Spence, the Scottish anthropologist, author, and poet, put it, they are to the Highland Scots as the wild fowl is to the domestic fowl. I remember them vividly from my childhood in the Western Isles — wild-looking families straggling along behind a handcart covered with a tarpaulin stretched across iron hoops. They called at the house to mend pots and kettles and to sharpen a few knives, and they seldom spoke. At night, they camped on the rough grass at the roadside; as children, we used to creep as close as possible in the dark to watch them around their fires, and to hear them sing. In winter, they settled in certain districts of Glasgow, Edinburgh, Inverness, and Dundee; in summer they turned up in Perthshire for the berrypicking, or wandered through the Highlands and islands as travelling tinsmiths or dealers in scrap. Many of them grew quite prosperous; my grandfather, who was a doctor in Glasgow, used to attend them regularly in their winter encampment at Vinegar Hill, in the east end of the city, and my mother remembered that they not only paid their bills promptly but quite often brought him generous presents. Since it was always much less difficult for the tinkers to cross the line that separated them, as travellers, from the working community than it was for the Romany gypsies in England, there has been no sudden crisis in Scotland over the status of Scottish travellers, but there have been plenty of instances of their being moved on by the police, and there is no doubt that the tinkers would welcome the same consideration that the English gypsies are likely to be given from now on.

The most curious thing about the tinkers is their language, for they speak either a Highland or a Lowland cant — a curious back slang deriving, in the case of Lowland cant, from a mixture of Scots and English words, and, in Highland cant, from the Béarlagair na Sáer, one of the secret languages of ancient Ireland. These secret languages were originally high-caste languages of particular sects, and were formed to conceal the secrets of the fraternity from other men. With time, as the status of the wandering smiths declined, the Béarlagair na Sáer declined, too, until it became a cover language, like the argots and flash languages used throughout the underworld to conceal the subject of conversation from any possible eavesdropper. Unlike Romany, the cant languages not only are very much alive among the tinkers today but contain a wealth of songs and stories, which in the past few years have been patiently recorded by the School of Scottish Studies, in Edinburgh — a tiny but immensely valuable department of the University that in recent years has been catching on tape the dwindling Scottish dialects and the oral literature of the Highlands. In many of the cant songs, policemen and farmers appear as the villains, or "black men," and in the stories there are many references to "burkers," a cant word that derives from the Edinburgh murderers Burke and Hare. (The tinkers believed that every night black coaches with muffled wheels, driven by black-coated men in "loony" hats, went out from Edinburgh over the highroads of Scotland looking for isolated tinkers, whose bodies they would supply to the medical schools.) The tinkers' fear of "flatties" — their word for non-tinkers — is much greater than any animosity the Scots feel toward them; in any event, they are much more adept than the English gypsies at moving in and out of civilization, and this is perhaps the reason for the contempt in which the gypsies hold them.

Gypsies, tinkers, travellers, vagrants — the more one looks into them, the more one discovers that civilization sets up its own discontents, and that the periphery is always inhabited either by those who are in flight from the center or by those who have been disinclined (perhaps from contentment, perhaps from suspicion) to move toward it. To be out, it seems to me, is not necessarily to be down, but at the same time it is difficult to see the inhabitants of the periphery as they are, without endowing them with self-conscious motives and turning them into champions of nonconformity. This they are not, but I have found in all of them an instinctive wariness — a feeling that if they were to move closer to the center, they would find themselves harassed by too many things beyond their ken or their control. The wariness persists, and is a kind of instinct. They cannot either own or master what they do not carry with them; legal rights — words written on paper — are not tangible enough for them to acknowledge as real.

In February of 1962, as a result of the fuss, the Ministry of Housing and Local Government issued a circular, directing county councils to arrange for a survey of the travelling population in their areas as soon as possible, and promising Ministerial support and assistance. It opened the way for the establishment of permanent sites where the gypsies could settle without fear of prosecution, and it conceded that "moving people off one unauthorized site and leaving them to find another is no solution, and no answer to the human and social problems involved." In addition, some private funds have been started for the resettlement of the travellers, and, all in all, it appears that the gypsies can look forward to a time of stability, with steady sites and, eventually, houses, schooling for the children, literacy, opportunities for work — all the comforts of a civilization that can, in fact, do little but gobble them up.

Sociologically, the problem is a practical one, and it looks as though it might be solved in a straightforward, practical way; the implications, however, remain. Whatever one may think of civilization, it becomes increasingly clear, from small instances like that of the English gypsies, that it is practically impossible to opt out. However stable may seem the form and substance of one's life, or way of life, the rug may suddenly be pulled out to make way for wall-to-wall carpeting, whether one wishes it or not. What moved me most in talking to the gypsies was their awesome timelessness; they lived, if they lived anywhere, in the recurring round of the seasons, not expecting things to get either better or worse, and accepting the small variations in their fate as they might accept the weather — as never predictable but, at the same time, never insupportable. Acts of God they allowed for, but Acts of Parliament they neither knew of nor could foresee, until suddenly they found themselves tumbled off the tiny plateau on which they had been quite happy to live. As one of my old mentors put it, " 'Twere not an *easy* life, Surr, but I can tell you true, we never wanted more as what we *had*, if we could be sure o' that. Now I sees the youngsters pesterin' for the *vardo* t' be changed for one o' them trailers, then the radio, an' all. Them's not gypsy ways, Surr. Amongst us, you knows the summer comes after the winter, an' you takes it as it comes. Let me not go blamin' nobody, but nowadays, when you gets given somethin', there's nobody as asks you whether you wants it or not."

Some time ago, an eviction order was served against a group of gypsy families living on a site that they had used for years but that was required urgently for a housing development. One cold morning, a sergeant of police went to the site with an order to move, and when he had explained it carefully to the old gypsy who acted as spokesman for the others, the man looked up at him with an anxious face and said, "Tell us where to go, Guv'nor, and we'll go." I'm glad he didn't say it to me. "On" would have seemed to be the only possible reply.

Curiosity
(for M. M-M)

may have killed the cat; more likely
the cat was just unlucky, or else curious
to see what death was like, having no cause
to go on licking paws, or fathering
litter on litter of kittens, predictably.

Nevertheless, to be curious
is dangerous enough. To distrust
what is always said, what seems,
to ask odd questions, interfere in dreams,
leave home, smell rats, have hunches
does not endear him to those doggy circles
where well-smelt baskets, suitable wives, good lunches
are the order of things, and where prevails
much wagging of incurious heads and tails.

Face it. Curiosity
will not cause him to die —
only lack of it will.
Never to want to see
the other side of the hill,
or that improbable country
where living is an idyll
(although a probable hell)
would kill us all.
Only the curious

have, if they live, a tale
worth telling at all.

Dogs say he loves too much, is irresponsible,
is changeable, marries too many wives,
deserts his children, chills all dinner tables
with tales of his nine lives.
Well, he is lucky. Let him be
nine-lived and contradictory,
curious enough to change, prepared to pay
the cat price, which is to die
and die again and again,
each time with no less pain.
A cat minority of one
is all that can be counted on
to tell the truth. And what he has to tell
on each return from hell
is this: that dying is what the living do,
that dying is what the loving do,
and that dead dogs are those who do not know
that dying is what, to live, each has to do.

Propinquity

is the province of cats. Living by accident,
lapping the food at hand, or sleeking down
in an adjacent lap when sleep occurs to them,
never aspiring to consistency
in homes or partners, unaware of property,
cats take their chances, love by need and nearness
as long as the need lasts, as long as the nearness
is near enough. The code of cats is simply
to take what comes. And those poor souls who claim
to own a cat, who long to recognize
in bland and narrowing eyes a look like love,
are bound to suffer should they expect
cats to come purring punctually home.
Home is only where the food and the fire are,
but might be anywhere. Cats fall on their feet,
nurse their own wounds, attend to their own laundry,
and purr at appropriate times. O folly, folly
to love a cat, and yet
we dress with love the distance that they keep,
the hair-raising way they have, and easily blame
all the abandoned litters and torn ears
on some marauding tiger. Well, no matter;
cats do not care.

Yet part of us is cat. Confess —
love turns on accident, and needs
nearness; and the various selves we have

all come from our cat-wanderings, our chance
crossings. Imagination prowls at night,
cat-like among odd possibilities.
Only our dog-sense brings us faithfully homeward,
makes meaning out of accident, keeps faith,
and, cat-and-dog, the arguments go at it.
But every night, outside, cat-voices call
us out to take a chance, to leave
the safety of our baskets, and to let
what happens, happen. "Live, live!" they catcall.
"Each moment is your next! Propinquity,
propinquity is all!"

Frog Dream

Nightlong, frogs in the pool
croak out calamity till, wakeful,
I interpret each crooked syllable.

The sound is churlish, coarse —
frog notes grating out a hoarse
chorus of slow remorse,

as I do, in half-sleep,
until, drifting, I cannot keep
the dark from deepening,

or dream voices from becoming
peepers and grunters, churning
my madness over. The pool is lapping,

weed-streaked, in my head.
Frogs echo from the edges of the bed,
in the grieving voices of the long dead,

grudges long hidden in their old throats,
hauntings, water horror, hates.
Somewhere, shivering, daylight waits.

Later, I wake, in the sanity of dawn,
and walk to the pool, glassy under the sun.
What did I dream? The frogs have all gone down.

Wishes

Sudden silence, an angel passing over,
two saying the same word, simultaneously,
a star falling, the first fruit of the year,
the breastbone of the chicken, scraped and dry —
each an occasion to wish on, a wish given.

Easy enough for children, for whom to wish
is only a way of bringing a party closer
or acquiring pennies or cake, and for whose sake
we attend to teeth beneath stones and believe in magic,
not indulgently but somehow because
each time the silver coin appears where the tooth was,
the party seems quick in coming, and beggars ride
pell-mell over the countryside.

But for ourselves, with fewer teeth and no faith
in miracles or good angels, a falling star
is likely to be uncomfortable. Oh, we can ask for
new lives, more money, or a change of face,
but hardly seriously. The heart is lacking.
We know too much, and wishing smacks of daydream
and discontent — not magic. Anyway, we are wary
of strings and snags or, worse, that, once fulfilled,
the thing we wished for might be old and cold.

Yet still the children come, with serious
rapt faces, offering us wishes.

[193]

Take this wishbone, delicate where the breast was,
whitened now by the sun, stick-brittle.
Hold one stem of it, lightly, with your little
finger. I will hold the other.
Now make your wish, my love; but never tell.

And I? I always wish you well;
but here, in this poise before the fruit can fall,
or the star burn out, or the word dwindle,
before the hovering angel
flies out of mind, before the bone is broken,
I wish we wish the same wish, the unspoken.

What Bones Say

The skeleton
is hardly a lesson
in human nature.

Similarly, stones
are the bones of landscapes,
and yet trees blossom

in contradiction.
We are much more
than our brittle topography.

Nevertheless,
what is it
about bones and skull

that suggests a whole
compelling humanity?
The bones' statuary

pose, like handwriting,
the thin, helpless,
scrawled mortality?

Wise to keep
a skull in the cupboard,
not as warning

but as a bulwark
against disaster
or wild dreaming.

And you — it behooves you,
that you may dispense
with my passing madness,

to take fair note
of this ultimate:
a skeleton loves you.

VI

IV

Whoosh Whoosh Whoosh

WHERE sports are concerned, you could call me Ishmael. I am prepared to go to an arena of any shape or size almost anywhere at all if there is reasonable hope of a contest; and if on some village green a player should be missing, my coat is likely to be the first one off. I began with an addiction to marbles at an extremely early age, at least to an urchin's version of marbles which in Scotland was called "guttery," played as it was along the sidewalk gutters and lasting as long as the gutter did, or until somebody's marble disappeared down the natural hazard of a drain. Rugby and soccer I took in my boyhood stride; cricket and tennis followed naturally with the changing seasons, and fisticuffs fell into their rightful place in the social scheme of things. I attended the University of St. Andrews, where it would have been hard not to play golf. I shot crows, pigeons of flesh and clay, and bottles off a wall; I threw javelins, hammers, discuses and stones; I climbed trees, cliffs, mountains and church spires; and whenever I lacked companions, I would alone replay soccer matches I had seen or read of, easily assuming in rapid succession the twenty-two different identities of the players, and occasionally beating myself. I ripped the sports pages from my father's newspapers and hoarded them in the attic. Sports statistics dribbled from my head, and when I had driven my family half-mad, I took to plundering the memories of old men on street corners and listening tirelessly to their quavering accounts of "the great Welsh match of '07," or some such. My dreams and daydreams were veritable Olympic contests.

The appetite, I confess, has never left me. Playing or watching, it makes no difference to me; the excitement is as keen. I managed, at odd times during the war, to play rugby in South Africa, soccer in Ceylon, cricket in Vizagapatam, and field hockey against a team of Oman tribesmen on a baked ground within the walled city of Muscat, at the entrance to the Persian Gulf. Accordingly, my first visit to the United States seemed to me like stumbling on Mars — baseball, basketball, American football, trotting races, and the like, all to be seen for the first time, odd, unpronounced names to be rolled round the tongue, a vast, new sporting vocabulary to be acquired, and, eventually, the same wistful, head-shaking conversations with near-identical old men in gloomy bars. But in the United States, I never caught fire in quite the same way. Sports was too available, too diversified, too immaculate, and my attention tended to grow ragged. Twitching the television dial through the whole field of muscular endeavor has never approached the nervous pleasure of waiting out the week prior to a game in a constant lather of excitement and having in the end the whole nervous system wrung out and put to rest in the space of two hours.

It was not, in fact, until I settled in Spain that my old appetites were rekindled with proper, juvenile ferocity. I buried myself in the bullfight, watching, listening, reading, learning, getting to know the movements, the hazards, the styles, the deceptions, all with a towering passion, until I was holding my own with the old men once more; but for most of the time, they were shaking their heads and recalling the past almost to the exclusion of the present, and so I turned in time to see what else was being waged across the Iberian Peninsula.

There was plenty. Spaniards are by far the most hungry spectators I have ever come across. On any spring Sunday in Madrid, you can take in the cockfights in the morning, the bullfights in the afternoon, the soccer game in the early evening, and, with luck and strength, the jai-alai around dinner time. The Spaniards also play baseball, but I did not linger long over it, after reading an account of a game between a Spanish and an Italian team in which the scores and the number of errors all ran high into double figures.

I settled eventually for soccer, since Madrid has the best team in the world, and plays with joyful precision, and since, for once, I found myself free of the shadow of the old men, Spanish football having an undistinguished past and a dazzling present. Moreover, sports writers in Spain are pure poets, often quite literally so, since, cramped by censorship and the prevailing *malaise* under Franco, Spanish writers often take to sports reporting to turn an honest peseta. The bullfight critics are masters of rhetoric, but they have decided that the decline of the bullfight is absolute, and their commentaries are generally graceful longing for the bulls, bullfighters and bravado of yesteryear. The football reporters write positive odes in the newspapers, and in Madrid, I took the utmost pleasure in watching a game of a Sunday and then reading three or four lyrical accounts of it the following day, rich in metaphor, incantatory in praise.

Anthropologists ought to give more serious and prolonged attention to sports than they do; the history and preoccupations of the human race are profoundly wrapped up in them. In Scotland, we were always told that soccer began in the reign of James IV, when a few Scottish soldiers began to kick the head of a captured Englishman about the market-place. I doubt that seriously; but I spent some time in the Basque provinces in the north of Spain, and acquired a sporting passion for pelota, or jai-alai, a game which runs through endless variations, and which seems to me to be the closest candidate for the oldest game of all. Basques in fact claim that it was played against the wall of the Garden of Eden, Adam of course being Basque. At any rate, whether it is played with the long, basket-woven *chistera*, the leather glove, or the bare hand, it boils down to hitting a ball against a wall, a natural happening which, for sheer delight, can still keep a right-minded child enthralled for hours. I was recently reading an account of some of the Central American ball games which Columbus stumbled across, and they are not far from the Basque game in their essentials, with the marked exception that, in early versions of their game, it was not an uncommon occurrence to sacrifice the captain of the losing team to the gods, an impulse which lingers on in the minds of true spectators, though nowadays in a repressed form.

These days, though, the sports pages are too cluttered for my taste, and I am forced to pick and choose a bit. Give me any game involving the orb, the sphere, the leather and the pigskin and I am content; the rest can serve as occasional diversions. Spain quite recently invented what must be the newest game to gain international status, namely hockey on roller skates; but for my money, it could just as well have been left uninvented — I attended it once, and the noise of it entirely eliminated any possibility of muttering those knowledgeable asides that true spectators like me love to mutter. No, I feel that the canon is pretty well complete, and that, until we are able to walk on water, we'd be better employed in eliminating some of the more questionable fringe-contests, like mud-wrestling and pogo-stick racing, just to keep the statistics out of the reach of the computers.

One of the first things to disappear from my book, I have always thought, would be bicycle racing, an activity about which I have never been able to muster more than mild horror. But as accident has it, I came to rest, one spring in France, on the edge of the Pyrenees. At first, I found myself within easy reach of pelota, French rugby, and occasional games of soccer; but as June wore on and the winter games frittered out, I grew increasingly uneasy, for all that came to replace them in the expanses of French newssheet were photographs and biographies of slim heroes, each with his arm curled lovingly round the handlebars of his bicycle. Gradually I overcame my horror and grew curious; and as June wore on, and the best pelota players had all gone to play in Spain, I realized that bicycle racing was all I had. Everything had been cleared away to make room for the Tour de France, the enormous annual bicycle race round France, the mention of which tends to make Frenchmen roll their eyes like stage Frenchmen. I decided to give it my unwilling attention. It would have been hard not to. The cafés were already humming with it, and the baker who called every morning took it upon himself to give me a long, explanatory lecture in installments, well in advance, to tauten my expectations.

The Tour de France (I learned) is an extraordinary occurrence, not only because it preoccupies almost the entire French populace for the better part of a month, but also because it manages in its progress to cover a large part of the country itself and to give a goodly number of the French a first-hand look at it. The route changes every year, although the finishing line remains in Paris; and from prolonged study of the maps in various tradesmen's windows, I found that the current *carrière* would bring the whole circus to within a few kilometers of me. I decided that it would be churlish not to go. The old men in the village were ready enough with advice. "Go to the mountains," one of them told me. "Four years ago, I saw a rider — an Italian, it was — fall down a ravine. Magnificent!" But I was not eager to go to the mountains — I had been held up there a few weeks before for two hours, to wait for a small local bicycle race to pass. Out of that time, six minutes were occupied by the actual passing of the entourage, most of it composed of quite ordinary cars with bicycles on their roofs, and a brief swish of actual, living cyclists. More cars. More gendarmes. This time, I resolved to go to the nearest finish line (the race is divided into daily stages, or *étapes*), feeling that, from a bicycle racing point of view, to arrive might be better than to travel.

I had over a week to prepare myself, and I did so assiduously. What I found astonished me. I had imagined bicycle racing to be a relative youngster in the canon, and felt that I might be able to do without the old men. Not so. The first Tour de France, to my astonishment, took place in 1903, giving the activity a seniority which could allow it to rub shoulders respectably with most national pastimes. Moreover, the race has that finality about it that makes other even more adventurous bicycle contests shrivel in comparison. "There is only *one* Tour de France!" the baker kept repeating dramatically. When I said this to M. Cachet, the wry advocate whom I occasionally met in the village, he rolled his yellowed eyes upward and muttered.

In principle, bicycles have not changed very much since a certain Monsieur de Sivrac, just prior to the French Revolution, had the idea of putting wheels instead of legs on a hobby-horse he had made for his children; but bicycling remained more or less walking on wheels until another Frenchman, M. Galloux, made the first self-propelling machine in 1837. (Whether the Tour de France came about as a result of the French having invented the bicycle, or whether the French claim the invention of the bicycle as a result of having thought up the Tour de France, my village sources are too sketchy to ascertain.) Many weirdly shaped bicycles appeared in the first years; but the bicycle evolved steadily, helped amongst other things by the invention of the pneumatic tyre in 1845 by Mr. Dunlop, an English veterinarian; and by 1900, it had more or less taken the shape it now has, give or take a refinement or two. In the photographs I have seen of the early Tours de France, it is in fashion and in the art of photography that most of the changes have happened, only minimally in the design of bicycles. Bicycle racing, too, was common enough at the beginning of the century, but in a smallish way; the idea of a vast marathon which would make a circuit of the whole of France came, as such ideas invariably do, to the editorial staff of a sporting journal called *L'Auto,* in 1902. Its director, Henri Desgrange, took the whole project under his wing, and whipped up a regular fever of popular interest. He divided the Tour into a series of six *étapes*, Paris–Lyon–Marseille–Toulouse–Bordeaux–Nantes and back to Paris, covering in all a distance of 2,428 kilometers. He arranged for a rough kind of surveillance, and charged only ten francs entry fee. Each *étape* had its winner, but to determine the overall winner, Desgrange proposed a *classement general*, whereby the times of each rider over each stage would be toted up, a system of scoring which is still followed. The first Tour was won easily by a small, chunky chimneysweep called Garin, who came home with a staggering advantage of two hours and forty-nine minutes over the runner-up; but, more important for Desgrange, the race caused tremendous excitement, and, everywhere, people swarmed to see it pass. Desgrange, fortified by all this, resolved to make it an annual event; but the following year, he ran into horrendous obstacles. A mysterious automobile with a crew of four masked men attacked the riders in the early stages; between Sainte-Étienne and Marseille, at about three o'clock in the morning (in those days, the long stages of the Tour ran on through the hours of darkness, a practice soon discontinued), close to a hundred thugs, armed with stones and cudgels, lined the road and did considerable damage to the principals as they passed, all in the cause of one Faure, who was promptly disqualified; at Nîmes, the troupe was further assaulted with bottles, and Desgrange vowed he would have no more of the Tour de France. By this time, however, the public had him by the hair, and the Tour slowly grew into a French tradition, heavily supervised by judges, and refining itself all the time. Penalties were awarded, and additional point systems established. Desgrange also decided to vary the route even more extravagantly, reconnoitering the roads through the Pyrenees and deciding that, with the help of the Departement des Ponts et Chaussées, and with vast sums of money from his own journal, they could be made passable to the participants. The number of *étapes* was increased, their distance shortened; the overall distance covered went up to 4000, and later to 5000 kilometers; in 1908, 114 riders started. The leading cyclists became national figures — the Tour was won in 1907 and again in 1908 by an impulsive little cyclist called the Petit-Breton, who was apt to fly into fearful rages and attack the judges; it was won three times, twice before and once after the Great War of 1914, by Phillippe Thys, a record which stood until Luison Bobet won it three successive times, from 1953 on. The history of the Tour was, I found, crammed with statistics, just as impressive, just as improbably useless as those of other sports; it abounds in records, and is strewn with eccentrics (one wore the rich name of Oscar Egg). The old men filled me with quivering accounts of the three Pélissier brothers, only one of whom won the Tour, but all of whom were tremendously popular, and of the great Cricri, who competed eleven times, between 1906 and 1925, but who never won. Cricri was a blacksmith by trade, and made history by breaking the front fork of his bicycle on three separate occasions, carrying the machine to the nearest smithy and forging a new fork for himself before riding on. I cannot remember many more of the old men's tales; one has to grow up with heroes, one cannot acquire them suddenly.

As might have been expected, the manufacturers of bicycles took a precipitous interest in the Tour de France once it was under way, and soon formed their own teams, looking after the expenses and travelling arrangements of the members. Desgrange, however, never at loss for a new idea, formed national teams in 1930 (he remained the father of the Tour de France until his death in 1941). Another early innovation of Desgrange's was to have the Tour touch each frontier of France;

it began in 1906 with an incursion into Lorraine, then annexed by Germany, and now takes in Germany and Italy, as well as making small sallies into Belgium, Switzerland and Spain. For so long a contest (it begins from Rouen in mid-June and ends in Paris in mid-July), the margin is often surprisingly close: in 1956, the French cyclist Walkowiak won by only 1 minute 25 seconds over his nearest rival. The lead is likely to change hands from *étape* to *étape*, quite conspicuously, for the overall leader wears a canary-yellow jersey, the *maillot jaune*, as it is called, instead of his team shirt; and he must hand it over to anyone who wins the lead away from him. The year I was watching, Jacques Anquetil, the French captain (Jacquot, as I soon learned to call him) had won and kept the *maillot jaune* from the very beginning. Would he hold on to it? Would he carry it all the way to Paris? The old men looked grave. "The mountains" — they said — "The mountains will tell."

The finishing line of the seventeenth *étape*, the one I was to see, was at Pau, the capital city of Béarn. To get there, I had to start early in the day; for, in the afternoon, the police closed most of the roads near the route of the Tour to let the cyclists pass unmolested. In the local paper, I read a long list of regulations which warned me, amongst other things, not to throw anything on or near the route from an aeroplane or helicopter. (The memory of 1905 when at one point 125 kilograms of nails were spread along the road obviously still smarted amongst the *gendarmerie*.) At any rate, I was in Pau in plenty of time, time enough indeed to have watched the start on television, as most of the citizenry seemed to be doing; but I felt it would blunt my anticipation.

Pau, an old haunt of Henry of Navarre, is a clean, prosperous, well-groomed town, full, it seemed that morning, of brown-necked farmers in unfamiliar suits taking their money to the bank. I read that, during the nineteenth century, the English settled there in quantity — the French poet, Alfred de Vigny, met his English wife, one Lydia Bunbury, in Pau, while he was stationed there as a captain of infantry. The English must have been responsible for the prim gentility of the place, for its vast hydropathic hotels looking across to the Pyrenees, for some of its obvious civic pride. There is something about thermal towns, even about the word "thermal," which rubs me the wrong way — it seems to oblige me to feel good, to breathe deeply, to be aware of my lungs, to empty the water carafe at table. Pau, however, was less thermal than usual that morning. People stood about in knots, obviously discussing the Tour; waiters whistled; there was an audible buzz in the air. At lunch, I sat facing the Pyrenees, scribbled unevenly across the horizon, partly obscured by drifting mist. Even now, the cyclists were struggling up the colls and passes. The old men would be there to watch and shake their heads. It still seemed a strange dedication to me. I wondered what went through the riders' heads. Water, I guessed.

Just after two o'clock, people began to drift in a noticeable direction, and I drifted with them. We wound our way downhill past the railroad station, where the road had already been enclosed by wooden fences. Here, it would be hard to swing a cudgel or throw a bottle, it occurred to me. To put myself as close as possible to the finish line, I bought a ticket to a covered stand, at the cost of seven new francs. A small, hoarse man sold me an official programme, and with it, free and unsolicited, came a Western comic strip, a throwaway dedicated to the theory that, in any case, Algeria was useless to France since it was only a matter of time before we would all be using synthetic gasoline, a leaflet of women's fashion patterns, and a magazine, the pages of which could apparently be ripped out and played on any convenient phonograph. Musing on this odd twist in human communications, I took my concrete seat. The stand was already well-filled and noisy, the crowd well-laced with old men in berets and a noticeable number of children. Below and in front of me, empty gas containers divided the road down the middle, bearing blue and yellow banners, the official colors of the Tour de France. From my programme, I learned that the cyclists would come racing from my left, would pass the stands on my half of the road, and then would disappear for a last loop of two kilometers before flashing back from my right across the finishing line, which was painted on the other half of the road opposite me. I found I was behind a pillar, and changed my seat. The French always leave empty seats behind pillars, so that anyone can arrive late for anything and find a seat that will allow him to see at least half of what is going on. I sat down beside a gloomy-looking man, who nodded to me.

The finishing line itself bristled with assorted press and television cameras, and a small glass radio booth that was apparently in close touch with the cyclists, for every now and then a fat man in shorts and sandals squeezed out of it and informed us who was ahead when and where. This he did with great panache and enthusiasm, as though the achievement had been his. "Now they're really in the mountains," growled the man next to me. "That's what will tell, the mountains." He proved to be both knowledgeable and to the point, and, when we were not observing silence for the fat man, he underlined for me some of the finer points of Tour strategy. What mattered nowadays, he explained, were your team-mates; they could help you, if you were ahead, by making a barrier to keep the others back, or by making a hole for you to escape through. Each team, he told me, works out a complicated daily plan, which they have to sharpen up as they go along. For most of the way, the riders are content to stick together in platoons, but at various times, one, two, or three of them try to escape and stay ahead. The escape which is important, naturally, is the escape to the finish line. Some escaped too soon and fizzed out, he told me. "It's strength that counts," he concluded. "Jacquot has the strength. Except for Charly, he has the *maillot jaune* in his pocket." . . . Would Jacquot win today? I asked him. He shook his head. "Anquetil's not a mountain man. He'll stay with the pack and keep his time clean. No, today, you'll see, it'll be an Italian. Today's going to clean the race up and get rid of the sleepers. If Jacquot's still ahead tonight, we can all go home." Home, I decided firmly, was where I was going that night, wherever Jacquot was.

Fortified by my new knowledge, I sat back. The sun went in, and the fat man obediently removed his sunglasses in midphrase. A man in yellow overalls showered us with paper hats, advertising coffee. A car drove slowly past, carrying two little blond girls in Béarnais costume, perched on the edge of the back seat, their arms barely encircling several giant bouquets, which later they were to present to the winners. We clapped dutifully. The girls looked frightened. A Frenchman called Queheille, a veritable hiccup of a name, was in the lead, the fat man informed us. We nodded and waited. Waiting is an odd state of being. The imagination creates the anticipated event in such completeness that any sign of compliance from the reality has the nervous system jumping. Accordingly, we cheered jumpily when a workman on a bicycle cruised past. He grinned and waved at us.

"Papa, they are not going to come at all," said the small boy in front of me, quite firmly. I knew how he felt.

Three important-looking officials were adjusting a banner that had been suspended over the line. (Competitors never need feel important; the officials at sporting events always do that for them.) The sky darkened, and a sudden spray of rain fell, throwing the crowd in the open stands on the other side of the road into confusion. The cameramen shrouded their cameras and themselves in plastic. One of the little Béarnais girls began to cry. The fat man comforted her, and then told us that Busto had passed Queheille. We cheered. A thin, cold boy was led to the microphone, and played two numbers for us on an accordion. Since we were supposed to know who he was, we applauded. No seats remained in the stand, even behind the pillars. The gendarmes began to hurry stragglers off the track. The fat man came back at a trot. Busto was still ahead, he told us, fifty kilometers from the finish; but, more important, the caravan would arrive any minute.

The *caravan de publicité* is about the only one of M. Desgrange's ideas to which I took sharp exception; but nevertheless, it is part and parcel of the Tour, and is meant to provide the lighter entertainment. I waited for it with some misgivings.

Down the track to our left appeared three helmeted and goggled motorcyclists, looking like the messengers of death in Cocteau films. We applauded again; but I was unprepared for what followed. Flanked by bicycling outriders, a giant motorized pressure cooker swept benignly past us, broadcasting in full cry. A girl on its roof was urging us to buy similar pressure cookers, but of a smaller, human size. Following it came an oversized vacuum cleaner, also motorized, and after that, a yellow plastic truck with a man on top, hurling packages into the crowd. The boy in front of me caught one neatly and opened it. "It's coffee," he said in disgust, and promptly threw it back. His father hit him. In front of me, now, three or four cars-of-the-future were weaving from side to side down the road. The noise was deafening. Someone obviously more important and more soberly dressed took over at the microphone from the fat man, who went sadly back to his car and lay down on the seat. Queheille had the lead back. An Italian was second. A truck with a plastic-cup-throwing cowboy passed; then, most terrifying of all, a giant motorized insect spray, followed by a string of plastic insects, lying on their backs, magnified several thousand times and also motorized. A man in a yellow shirt, well known to everyone except me, came to the microphone to sing to us. We could not hear him, nor did we care, for by now we were watching *le grand supercar,* an elongated bus filled with girls, who were giving away more paper hats. I dreaded what would come next. I was right. It was a truck-sized toothpaste tube, with a cowboy waving to us through a door in its side. We had come a long way from the age of the bicycle. O Commerce! — I thought — O France!

Now, the vacuum cleaner drove back on the other side; we were to see the whole caravan for a second, dizzying time. A beer wagon had stopped in front of us, with a friendly-looking type on top, distributing beer. The thin boy with the accordion was back at the microphone, unfortunately, as it happened, for simultaneously, a truck crept past, bearing a girl in a plastic cage, also playing an accordion. Busto was still leading, 17 kilometers from Pau. The man next to me, miraculously, was asleep.

A car with some bicycle wheels birling on its roof raised my hopes, but they were quickly dashed by a posse of seven motorcyclists, who swept past, standing on the saddles of their machines, with a car made up as a helicopter on their tail.

The beer wagon had stopped opposite us on the other side, its cheerful occupant passing out bottles to the cameramen. One of them apparently wanted a bottle-opener as well; the beerman, dropping his amiable mask, indicated that he could find one for himself, and a savage argument developed, which we enjoyed hugely. A fifteen-foot-high yellow plastic giraffe with bicycle feet diverted us momentarily.

"I know, there's a man inside," said the boy in front. I liked him.

At that moment, the girl in the plastic cage, who proved to be lady accordion champion of the world, graciously descended to play for us. The motorcyclists came back, sitting down now, looking fully satisfied, as if they were inwardly aware of the motorcycle's superiority to the bicycle. The Tour de France for them was no great hardship. The man beside me woke up. "Where is Charly Gaul?" he asked me suddenly. (Charly Gaul is a Luxembourgian cyclist who won the Tour in 1958, an event then generally regarded as a happy omen for the President of the French Republic.) I was able to tell him that, at last hearing, Charly Gaul had been lying forty-fifth. He shrugged. "Then he's finished," he muttered. An enormous motorized plastic pigeon passed the giraffe going in the opposite direction. Some normal-looking cars with bicycles on their roofs began to come in, and my hopes rose again. This time they were able to stay up. Queheille was not only ahead, he was approaching the outskirts of Pau, the microphone told us. We all stood up.

Now, the gendarmes began to behave like policemen, and the tracks were cleared off once and for all. A woman adjusted the dresses of the Béarnais girls and armed them with the bouquets. The accordions were silent, and the plastic animals had disappeared. Dusty cars came in and immediately wheeled off the track into a park. The cameramen squinted through their sights. We craned our necks down the road. It was close to five o'clock. The man beside me stretched and yawned. "It's all over," he said. "If Charly Gaul's not in the first three, then it's all over." For me, to the contrary, it was just beginning.

The roar began far away and rippled in waves towards us; then, sure enough, over the top of the fences appeared three white-capped heads, sweeping round the bend. After the animals, they seemed to me to be going at a tremendous speed. Two cyclists in gray jerseys, wheel to wheel, were keeping back a third with a green stripe round his middle. They were crouched over their handlebars, pumping the pedals furiously. They zipped towards us, whoosh whoosh whoosh, and were past, out of sight on the right. We were all cheering wildly. "That's the sprint," yelled my neighbor. "That's what kills them!" I had barely time to get my head round again before a cluster of heads appeared at the bend and were on us, whoosh whoosh whoosh whoosh whoosh, a group of seventeen or so, although nobody without an electric eye could have counted them at that speed.

Catching a blur of yellow in their midst, I concluded that Anquetil was with them. A cameraman fell off his pedestal. The microphone was announcing something none of us could hear. Another roar, and round the bend came another platoon, almost double the last, flashing past us like an extraordinary machine, multicolored, blurred. Then everyone's head jerked in the other direction; the finish. From the right came the three leaders, even faster than before, having completed their two-kilometer lap. The green stripe had put a wheel in front of the other two, and whizzed across the line a fraction ahead, raising his arm in salute. All three braked at once and were immediately swallowed up by swarms of officials and men wearing towels. Whoosh from the other side, a solitary blue jersey. I wanted to find out which was Queheille, but nobody knew. We stood and roared. Whoosh whoosh whoosh whoosh whoosh, and the column containing Anquetil and his yellow jersey had crossed the line. They dismounted in a body and walked, like people who had not walked for a long time, which was indeed true, toward an enclosure, through embraces, backclappings and questions, handing their bicycles to helpers, glad to be rid of them. From the other direction came a solitary, mud-stained rider, bleeding from one knee, and lacking his back tire, which he wore round his neck. Clank clank clank, he passed us. The beer-purveyor, his good cheer back, bustled in the enclosure, offering beer to everyone. Whoosh whoosh whoosh came another group from the left. Whoosh whoosh whoosh whoosh went the previous one across the line. Clank clank came the bleeding solitary. "Only seven to come," said a man behind me. How he knew, I could not imagine. I noticed the fat man, in a suit by this time, trying to clear a way to the winner's side, dragging the two little Béarnais girls in his wake. He worked them in, and they got rid of their bouquets, obviously relieved. It had been a long day for them. The winner, who proved to be a Belgian, kissed them both, and we cheered again, or at least redoubled our cheering. Queheille had been third, my neighbor informed me. Whoosh whoosh went another pair, Italians this time, with a British cyclist pedalling agonizingly at their backs. The cyclists seemed all to have disappeared, but the Belgian was still there, with his flowers. I caught sight of Jacquot talking to the cheerful beerman, wiping his hands on his yellow jersey. The lady accordion champion of the world was being brought forward to present something else to the Belgian. She kissed him, and the yellow giraffe reappeared behind her. My neighbor shook my hand, and prepared to leave. "It's all over," he yelled. "Jacquot has it in his pocket." I waited a moment, and followed him. As I left, someone handed me a packet of coffee. I kept it.

On the way to the station, I stopped at a café. There, on the television set, I saw the little Béarnais girls again, and the yellow giraffe, and the fat man; and I saw the Belgian make a leisurely tour in front of the stands, carrying his flowers. Que-heille came forward to tell us that it had been a fine race, and that he preferred the mountains to any other stage of the Tour. He did not even look tired. His trainer was clapping him on the shoulder, obviously pleased to be there. Then the lady accordion champion of the world came forward to tell us that she and all the others would be seeing us later that evening, in town.
Not me.

As I reached home, a warm dusk was gentling the tall poplars, and General de Gaulle was speaking on the radio about the future of Algeria. I wondered if Charly Gaul was listening. Probably not. If he had any sense, he'd be having a hot bath and a decent sleep. The following day, after all, he had another 207 kilometers of hard pedalling, all the way to Bordeaux. I hoped he was in bed early, dreaming of giraffes and yellow jerseys.
On the table, I found a note from an old Russian gentleman who lives in a neighboring village. He would be delighted, it said, if I would come over and play croquet with him quite

soon, whenever I wanted. I'll go, of course. I like talking to him, and, after all, it's a game. The only trouble is that the village is a bit far to walk. Well, I may even buy a bicycle, who knows. I like that *whoosh* sound.

The Seventh Day

NOTHING depresses me as much as other people's Sundays, those long, lame, aimless stretches of waste, sad time, like bad habits, or a kind of doom. When I was a child, I used, every now and again, to have a very telling vision (I was prone to visions of a most matter-of-fact sort) of God resting on the seventh day, sprawled across the universe, pleasantly exhausted, playing with a smile, pleased at the way the world had gone, quietly happy. Everything, I suppose, depends on how you construe "and he rested on the seventh day," but to read it as an Absence rather than a Presence seems to me a drastic failure in understanding.

The shape of days is settled at a very early point in life, mainly by what we do with them. Mondays begin and Fridays end, Saturdays celebrate, but Sundays — Sundays are suspended in nothingness, left to the devices of whoever wishes to give them shape, neutral zones in time subject to various interpretations, sacred to miscellaneousness. After an eventful week, nothing is supposed to happen on Sunday; it is a day that confronts us with our own fragile mortality, requiring us to content ourselves with the simple business of being alive, a primal matter that appears to consternate most people to the point of distraction. If all this were properly realized, we might conceivably take a great deal more trouble than we do with the week, to give it pith and moment; and we would have to decide what we wanted Sunday to be, or at least to appear, especially to children.

I happen to love Sundays, an accident of circumstance which derives quite clearly from my childhood. Although I grew up in Scotland, where Sunday is the most shuttered, barren, forbidding and proscriptive of all days, I was saved from the general inertia by the fact that my father was a minister, and that Sunday, instead of being a piece of temporal punctuation, was the Great Climax of the week. On Saturday evenings, we were shovelled out of the way to leave my father alone to wrestle with his own private angel. I still remember with awe the silence of the study, the feeling of sheer thinking that emanated from it like a tangible cloud. I still remember the sharp edge of anticipation in which Saturday expired, like a frail younger brother, and Sunday loomed.

Sunday in Scotland is the Sabbath, a day you might easily mistake for Doomsday if you were not used to it, a day that barely struggles into wakefulness. Shops, pubs, cinemas, cafés, bandstands, anywhere, in fact, where people with social inclinations might encounter one another, are not only shut but sealed — at least, if not literally, they feel as if they should be.

Houses are as silent as safes, and silence is as safe as houses; bottles are not only stoppered but locked; and, in the appropriate season, you can hear a leaf thud to the ground. Ecclesiastical ghosts stalk the countryside; the weather is the only noticeable happening.

Even animals absorb the mood of the day, and lie sluggishly in corners, minding their own drowsy business; people pull down the blinds in their heads, and listen hazily to bells tolling, nostrils twitching hopefully for a whiff of dinner. The guilty feel more guilty, the righteous more righteous, and the children, abandoned to their own tiny devices, wonder where life has gone, scrawling their way through homework which at least gives them the faint, quivering hope that Monday may come, that the world has not ended after all.

But not in our house. As soon as Sunday dawned, gray though it usually was, we sprang into life, aware that the week was about to go off like a rocket. We breakfasted in the dining room instead of the kitchen, and always more handsomely than usual; we groomed ourselves, and nipped into the garden for a sniff at the day. My father always turned up for breakfast, looking suitably serious and responsible — through the week he was a parent, but on Sunday he came down in clerical black, an emissary from a remote but marvellous planet, and we watched him with proper awe.

Church came at eleven; and since we were four children, one of us was always allowed to stay behind. We hugged this privilege, traded it, looked forward to it, saved up for it, took it for what it was, a gift of time. In the kitchen, my mother laid down the bones of lunch; in the study, my father assembled his notes, and absorbed the last of the silence. He left well ahead of us; we always said good-bye to him as though we might never see him again, which in a sense was true, for when he appeared in the pulpit, he was transmogrified, not at all the same person who had been buttering toast a brief hour before. We clambered into our best clothes, dealt out a miscellany of Bibles and pennies, and were off at the first clang of the bell, wheeling into our pew like a small, proud army.

I cannot even now decide which I liked best, my off-days at home, or my official, churchgoing days. Church was certainly never dull. I gaped at the incredible hats, the grave faces; I checked and cross-checked who was there, who was not; I grew to love the woodwork, with a microscopic eye; I listened to the bubbling, breathy wheeze of the organ, and fell in love with a succession of sopranos in the choir; and I gazed at my father, not perhaps hearing what he said, but believing it all faithfully in advance, desperate with love and admiration. I scanned the hymns and the paraphrases, and when the service worked itself up to the benediction, I felt it fall on me like some marvellous light, and walked out into the air with a sense of having been changed into something very different from my grubby, workaday, ink-stained, stone-kicking self.

But the off-days — left alone in the house for an incredible hour and a half, with nobody to say yes or no — these were probably the days. I used to listen for the gate clicking behind the church party, and then I was off, running through the rooms, trying on my father's tile hat, playing the grand piano with *both* pedals pressed down, tearing into the attic, riffling through the bookshelves in search of Something I Didn't Know Yet, wondering whether I might try shaving at the age of nine, writing with a real pen, stirring the soup as I had been told, darting into the garden, walking with a limp and a stick, acting out how many crowded, stored-up fantasies, reading letters which weren't mine, gaping at photographs of the First World War, then racing round to be sure everything was back in its

place before the gate clicked again, and the door burst open
and spilled in the virtuous, churchgoing survivors. I told them
what I had done — "Nothing, really!" — and they reported that
Mr. Rodgers had asked where I was, that Miss Smart had got
the hiccups — endless, ludicrous happenings. And then lunch.

Lunch on Sundays was for us a ritual of sheer joy, a giddy,
unbounded celebration. We wriggled out of our suits, put them
away, and came down to a meal that always smacked of
manna; it simmered on the stove until my father arrived, re-
stored to his human shape, full of smiles, jokes and fulfillment.
We sat round the table until the last possible moment, well-fed
and flushed with good will, small lords of the week, planning
away the sacred afternoon. On wet days, we put on Hamlet,
did circuses or jigsaw puzzles, chewed gum illicitly, and paged
through encyclopaedias. Most often, we went for walks, all in
different directions, climbing neat, comfortable hills, accom-
plishing military campaigns and lone sagas of heroic adventure.
Sundays gave us our heads, and we took them and ran wildly
away with them, as if they were balloons.

In the evenings, as we nuzzled closer to the fire, trimming
the ends of our homework, the prospect of Monday troubled
us not at all, for we knew that it was only the first, drab step on
a ladder that always led to Sunday, when our crumpled busy
worlds could be counted on to burst open and rainbow down,
when we would all be present at what was, for us, a ritual
celebration, not so much of God or John Knox or the Presby-
terian virtues, but of the simple, exuberant fact that we were a
family.

The odd thing about those days is that I don't think we were
particularly religious — instead we were a fairly standard mixture of good and bad, wild and warm, lucky and terrified, like

all children. God we knew as a friend of *our* father, his Boss in some incalculable way; and though a goodly company of angels and prophets ran through our dreams, they seemed no more real or awesome than Hamlet or the Bad Brownies. What we did absorb, in mystical osmosis, through our pores rather than our ears, was a curious and deep reverence for things, a feeling which hung like an aura over our Sundays, and which has stayed with me, so that I still look on Sunday as a ritual day, a day on which the meals are to be savored more than usual, the air to be breathed more deeply, when the afternoons are to be luxuriated in, the evenings to be meditated away mellowly.

This has stayed with me, even through the war, when there were no Sundays, and even although, since I work at home, Sunday is not externally different from the six other, run-of-the-calendar days. To me Sunday stands on a dais slightly raised above the level of the week; and even if the gods of one's childhood are argued into thin air, there are always others to be celebrated in their places, always new rituals to set up against the swirl of time.

Perhaps it was in reaction to the drear and mournful Scottish Sabbath that ours were so exuberant; but now, when I go back to Scotland, and suddenly see how heavily time must have been hanging outside our garden wall, I begin to realize how lucky we were, and how wise was my father. But the Sabbath, even more so now, seems to me to be a disastrous misinterpretation, from the point of view of religion, or of psychology, or anything else, a wet blanket of a day, celebrating nothing, signifying less. On the Sabbath, Scotland pulls the covers over its head, and groans away the useless silence.

In Spain, I have discovered a Sunday after my own heart, which goes wild in the way ours once did, and seems to me a much more expansive, human interpretation of what God would have liked to do with the seventh day, after making something as complex and exacting as the world. Spain saves up for its Sunday, and spends more than it has saved. Everyone dresses up to the nines, goes to early Mass to give thanks in advance, bursts out, smiling widely, and goes about the business of making the day more memorable than last week, which in its time was more memorable than the week before.

Sunday lunches outstrip even the golden meals of my boyhood, and last into the languorous late afternoon. Time for a walk, perhaps, before the bullfight or the soccer match, time for wine before the crowded, ebullient evening, least time of all for the minimum of sleep before Monday begins — slow, pesetaless Monday, when the week staggers to its feet and takes aim. The target? Sunday, with God in His hearty, human, all-giving heaven — a day on which there is more wine than glasses, more feet than shoes, and more kisses than lips.

I am half-inclined to measure the countries of the world by what they make of their Sundays; and if I had my way, I would have all the Scots transported to Spain, and swallowed up once and for all in the sheer good humor of one Spanish Sunday, so that they flew home singing, and broke out their bottles, bagpipes, and brightest bonnets, and hung John Knox in the cupboard where he began, and should have remained, as a meagre, moping ghost, in a dun nightgown of his own loose skin.

Days, one ought to know, are not to be wasted; and so Sunday deserves more than crosswords and aimless walks, casual visits, cold meals. It deserves to be, not a No-day, but a Yes-day. Perhaps it is time we shouted down the Lord's Day Observance Society, and took the Sabbath into our own hands, dressing up for it as we might for a fancy-dress ball, toasting it in elixirs, keeping it clear of obligations other than the one we have to the fact that we are (luckily) alive at all.

To a Child at the Piano

Play the tune again; but this time
with more regard for the movement at the source of it,
and less attention to time. Time falls
curiously in the course of it.

Play the tune again; not watching
your fingering, but forgetting, letting flow
the sound till it surrounds you. Do not count
or even think. Let go.

Play the tune again; but try to be
nobody, nothing, as though the pace
of the sound were your heart beating, as though
the music were your face.

Play the tune again. It should be easier
to think less every time of the notes, of the measure.
It is all an arrangement of silence. Be silent, and then
play it for your pleasure.

Play the tune again; and this time, when it ends,
do not ask me what I think. Feel what is happening
strangely in the room as the sound glooms over
you, me, everything.

Now,
play the tune again.

The Transformations:
Notes on Childhood

C HILDHOOD, especially for a poet, is irresistible; his preoccupation with it would be completely incomprehensible
to a child. From the vantage point of his aging consciousness,
he finds himself, either through the eyes of his own children
or through sudden green transformations of memory, dissolv-
ing into these states of pure trance (states which he can never
forgive children for being unaware of), in which a single day
is a clear, prismatic present, when a glass of water, instead of
being a complex molecular structure, or a lucid piece of punctuation in a disordered chain of consequences, or an image in
which the whole world is somehow reflected, stands on the
table as nothing more or less than a glass of water, wondrously,

needing no reason or excuse for its existence. I like nothing more than to listen to people talking about their childhood. Bit by bit, they work their way through a morass of judgment and sophisticated afterthought, psychiatric blah, and scholastic roughage until they reach, if they are lucky, an unencumbered point of pure memory — a day, an instance, a happening, tragic perhaps, comic more likely, but quivering with sheer life, pure and inexplicable, like the glass of water.

What, in fact, do we save from childhood? On the surface, a miscellaneous collection of odds and ends: birth certificates, because they are so permanently necessary to prove that we exist at all; baby shoes, perhaps, because we cannot otherwise conceive of having been no more than eighteen inches tall; fluffy photographs of our bald, naked beginnings; stamps, shells, feathers, skeletons; thumbed books about gnomes, brownies, and heroes; tickets, scraps, lists, dried leaves. These are the relics and the gravestones, and are meant, in their tiny, wizened way, to evoke an aura, to suggest a state of grace; yet how shrivelled they are, as they lie in a curiously smelling drawer, waiting for the day when we are courageous enough to cremate them.

Childhood is by definition a never-never land, a place where we have unaccountably been without knowing it, a nowhere which took up all our time before we realized what time was. Children drift through their sky-blue days without any feeling of being in motion; landmarks like birthdays loom on the far-away, blurred horizon, and move so slowly that it seems they will never arrive. When I was a child, even to wait for the next day was agonizing to me; in prospect, the night seemed so long and impassable, until I grew into a faith in the fact that I *would* wake up in a different, new-made day. For children, the future is so remote that it scarcely exists at all; the odd thing about growing up is the way in which the landmarks begin to move, faster and faster, until they are whizzing past like telephone poles. And the principal irony of childhood lies in the fact that we wander through it in an almost complete daze, unselfconscious, open-eyed, until we find ourselves gawking back at it from an age of realization, as somewhere we have been without noticing, wondering how we managed to pass the unwitting time.

But still, when we come to look at childhood, at the remove of judgment, do we see it at all? Or, instead, do we somehow accommodate it into the life we have later arrived at, trimming it to fit, forgetting its oddness and contradiction? I listen to people telling their childhood, and wonder, not just at the fact that they ever were children, but more, whether the versions of their own childhood they have come to believe in bear any relation to the small, vanished selves they have left behind. Childhood seems to them no more real than old movies, the aftermath of a story they were once told but of which they have only the vaguest recollection.

What most people do, I suspect, is save for their later, fullgrown days a few places, a few set pieces, a welter of anecdote (which over the telling years grows more and more original) to serve as memory whenever it becomes necessary to explain away the unconscious, missing years. Of the original, in its original form, little remains. It is, after all, better to decide that one had a happy childhood than to admit one had a relatively unconscious one, better to select the choicest places, the most fruitful occasions, and make of them a serviceable tapestry to suit the blandest of biographers. Or it may be just as serviceable to look back on childhood as the point where everything went wrong, to find, under the unruffled surface, monsters and nightmares. No wonder psychoanalysts take so long

to get to the bottom to find the early secret, the original sin —
childhood is in fact bottomless, and has its own strange scale.

The principal difference between childhood and the stages
of life into which it invisibly dissolves is that as children we
occupy a limitless present. The past has scarcely room to exist,
since, if it means anything at all, it means only the previous
day. Similarly, the future is in abeyance; we are not meant to
do anything about it until we reach a suitable size. Corre-
spondingly, the present is enormous, mainly because it is all
there is — a garden is as vast as Africa, and can easily become
Africa, at the drop of a wish. Walks are dizzying adventures;
the days tingle with unknowns, waiting to be made into
wonders. Living so utterly in the present, children have an
infinite power to transform; they are able to make the world
into anything they wish, and they do so, with alacrity. There
are no preconceptions, which is why, when a child tells us he
is Napoleon, we had better behave with the respect due to a
small emperor. Later in life, the transformations are forbidden;
they may prove dangerous. By then, we move in a context of
expectations and precedents, of past and future, and the present, whenever we manage to catch it and realize it, is a shifting,
elusive question mark, not altogether comfortable, an oddness
that the scheme of our lives does not quite allow us to indulge.
Habit takes over, and days tend to slip into pigeonholes, accounted for because everything has happened before, because
we know by then that life is long and has to be intelligently
endured. Except that, every now and again, one of these moments occurs, so transcendent in its immediacy, so amazing in
its extraordinary ordinariness, that we get a sudden glimpse of
what childhood was all about and of how much the present has
receded before a cluttered past and an anxious future. In these

odd moments, the true memory of childhood dawns. The glass of water is, amazingly, a glass of water.

Quite often, there comes a time when we try deliberately to recover childhood, revisiting a place, a house, a garden. Perhaps it would be better not to; almost inevitably it is a puzzlement, if not a downright disappointment. How wizened it is, how shrunken, how small, how unlike the mysterious nowhere we imagined we inhabited! I recall once revisiting a seaside village in Scotland where I lived as a child, a small harbor town I had gone over lovingly in what I thought was my memory, telling it house by house, hearing the high tides thud against the seawall in my sleep. Yet, when I walked around the harbor, I wondered how I could ever have been carried away by it, even in dream, so ordinary, small, and grubby it was, so unglowing, a poor stage for the wonders I remembered as having happened there in my small, broody days. The particular tree I made a profession of climbing had become only one in a series of trees, not, as it was then, the only tree in the world, Ygdrasil. And the people who remembered me now had to take their place in the context of time; they no longer belonged to the towering world of unchanging legend that my child's eyes and ears had appointed them to. They were mortal. "Don't change unless I tell you to!" cries the child to the world; and the world, instead of replying, goes quietly about its business of changing us, of turning what once was called growing up into growing old.

My own childhood, now that I look back on it with the proper distrust, seems to have been not extraordinary, for all childhoods are that, but a peculiar mixture of earth and air, of the practical and the impossible. My father was a minister of the church and moved and breathed with an extraordinary reverence for things, a reverence we absorbed simply by being in the same house with him. He did not speak often; when he did, I used to listen to him with the proper astonishment. My mother, on the other hand, was a doctor of medicine, and ran her doctoring and her household with a ribald, go-ahead, down-to-earth directness. They were, for us children, like the North and South Poles. Heaven knows what strange equilibrium they achieved, but we children were the fruit of it, and we spun dizzily from one to the other, from the no-nonsense bustle of the kitchen and surgery at one end of the house to the quiet, smoke-laden, book-lined study at the other. In between was a long corridor, our limbo. Outside was the world. Even now, I simplify, for it was never so neat; I cannot even remember whether or not there was a corridor, but there should have been. Along it, we were always in motion, disobedient this side of disaster, but busy with the odd variety of our existence.

Nevertheless, for all our participatory joy, we looked up at our parents as if we were underwater and they in the air, seeing them from below, larger than life, through the wavering prismatic surface, yet unable to call from our swaying, crystal-clear world to theirs. Our elements were separate, different. My mother was too busy to reach us, my father too shy; and we, for our part, with wonder bubbling from our mouths, did not know how to speak the first word. Even across time, nothing has broken that thin, taut meniscus, that soundless, separating glass. There comes a time when it is too late to begin talking, even to oneself.

Scotland we hardly noticed; it was no more than weather and landscape, and we lived, if we lived anywhere at all, between garden and water, in a mud-stained leaf-smelling round of errands and holidays, our feet on the ground, our heads firmly in the clouds. At school, among our friends, we spoke the local dialect bluntly and boisterously; at home, we clipped it to suit the household. As a minister's family, we had an odd immunity from the strata of local society. We knew — and played with — everyone from the snotty-nosed farm children to the starched and proper county families, who envied us our worldliness. We knew worse words than they did, and used them judiciously. At the same time, however, we were foreigners, never quite belonging anywhere; we had books at home, and things obviously went on as a matter of course in our house which never would have occurred in the rest of the town — blood and sermons, blessings and bandages.

I hovered for years between the surgery and the study, trying to decide whether I was cut out for the pulpit or the operating room; but I solved my dilemma by plunging into the mysterious countryside and by playing endless fantastic games over which, at least, I had control. The poles were noise and silence; I ran wild during the day, and in the evening I crept into the deep silence of books, unreachable. All of us kept passing and repassing one another along the length of the corridor, some on their way to burst, hungry and shouting, into the kitchen, others to tiptoe into the study, breath held, shoes in hand.

And yet, none of this is quite what I remember; it is rather the context and setting for my remembering. I recall, some years ago, taking a long voyage under sail across the Atlantic and passing the night watches — which we took alone at the wheel, under the enormous processes of the sky — by applying my memory to a particular place, a particular day, a particular time. With time — and there was plenty — I found I could recover whole periods of my life which I had not thought of since they happened. I remembered the names of those who had been in my school classes; and, with practice, I could take long walks over stretches of lost country, scrutinizing farms, trees, landmarks on the way; so that, night after night, perched alone in the middle of the Atlantic, I replayed most of my childhood like an endless movie, not for the sake of finding anything out, but, as the English say, just because it was there. It seemed particularly appropriate, for then I had no context, save for the sea, the dark, and the innumerable repetitive stars; and I sat under them, saying over to myself long lists of names I was not aware I knew — Kirkmaiden, Catyins, Linglie, Yarrowford, Pirnmill, Altgolach, Imacher, Windygates — amazing myself with their sound, seeing each place vividly in my mind's eye. It was then I realized that my childhood was not lost; all that was required to recover it was the dimension of amazement.

In the eyes of children, anything can happen, for so little has happened before; for us, at a remove, we know what is likely and what impossible, and so our propensity to astonishment is much less. Moreover, we tend to forget, as Christopher Fry says, that we were born naked into a world of strange sights and sounds, not fully clothed, in a service apartment, with a copy of the *Times* in our hand. This is why some of the afterthought we apply to the world of children — the books they ought to read, the things they should be interested in, the ways in which they should pass their time — is often preposterous and seems to assume that children are our idea, not theirs. Children are interested in anything except, possibly, the things they are expected to be interested in; and we might as well lay our world open to them and let them make off with whatever improbable treasure they discover for themselves.

I suppose the difficulty lies in deciding exactly who children are, in seeing them mistakenly as small replicas of ourselves, or as raw material, or as undersized animals, or as a race of miniature entertainers, or trainees, or even as income-tax deductions. I prefer to regard them — and, indeed, they demand to be regarded — as sudden visitors from an unlikely planet, frail, cogent messengers from a world which we know by name but have lost sight of, little people who are likely not only to amuse and amaze us but to remind us that life is long, and that they, as much as we, have a right to their own version of it. The mistake we mostly make is to encumber children with the versions we retain of our own childhood, to imagine that what would have been good for us, as we think we were then, will be good for them, as we think they are now. Children are entitled to their otherness, as anyone is; and when we reach them, as we sometimes do, it is generally on a point of sheer delight, to us so astonishing, but to them so natural.

The Spiral

The seasons of this year are in my luggage.
Now, lifting the last picture from the wall,
I close the eyes of the room. Each footfall
clatters on the bareness of the stair.
The family ghosts fade in the hanging air.
Mirrors reflect the silence. There is no message.
I wait in the still hall for a car to come.
Behind, the house will dwindle to a name.

Places, addresses, faces left behind.
The present is a devious wind
obliterating days and promises.
Tomorrow is a tinker's guess.
Marooned in cities, dreaming of greenness,
or dazed by journeys, dreading to arrive —
change, change is where I live.

For possibility,
I choose to leave behind
each language, each country.
Will this place be an end,
or will there be one other,
truer, rarer?

Often now, in dream,
abandoned landscapes come,
figuring a constant theme:

[237]

Have you left us behind?
What have you still to find?

Across the spiral distance,
through time and turbulence,
the rooted self in me
maps out its true country.

And, as my father found
his own small weathered island,
so will I come to ground

where that small man, my son,
can put his years on.

For him, too, time will turn.